David

from

Mom

Other books by the same author

BIRD THOU NEVER WERT

SORRY I STIRRED IT

*more than
100 forays,
advances, skirmishes,
ambushes,
victories, cop-outs,
standoffs and
outflankings
in the
funny business
of living*

HALF THE BATTLE

SIMON
AND
SCHUSTER
NEW YORK

Bill Vaughan

For, in the order of their appearance,
Kirk and Ellen

ACKNOWLEDGMENT

Much of this book appeared originally in *The Kansas City Star* and is used here with its permission and generous cooperation. Readers of other newspapers may have encountered some of these pieces, which are distributed by the Bell-McClure Syndicate.

Contents

Why are we here?

CONSTRUCTIVE CRITIC: *How come you are able to think up such punk titles for your books?*

ME: *Just a knack, I guess. Some people have it; some don't. Shakespeare was terrible on titles, although very good in other ways. Can you imagine calling a play "Hamlet" instead of "How to Avoid Probate in Denmark"?*

CONSTRUCTIVE CRITIC: *Shakespeare aside, the big thing to remember is that for your kind of book a good title is half the battle.*

ME: *You mean half the battle is a good title?*

CONSTRUCTIVE CRITIC: *Put it any way you want.*

So I will thank the Constructive Critic for the good title and overlook whatever it was he meant by "your kind of book."

Beyond that, "Half the Battle" seems apt for this particular book. It comes when I am halfway through the battle of life. Exactly halfway if I live to be 104.

It is a good, or at least a traditional, time to take stock of the battle and file some sort of position paper. Here, then, are records of forays, advances, skirmishes, ambushes, victories, cop-outs, standoffs and outflankings.

In addition it might be pointed out that "Half the Battle" fits this book because it tells of no grand crusades nor total commitment of forces, and claims no ultimate triumphs.

✳✳✳✳

NAME, RANK AND
SERIAL NUMBER

Or: the definitive life of an indefinite man

✳✳✳✳

The trouble with a lot of books is that it's only after two or three hundred pages that you feel you are really getting to know the author, and there is nothing worse than being written at by somebody you don't know.

Some people who write books you never get to know until they marry your sister or come to town to make a speech. Others remain a mystery until you study them in college and find out things you always wondered about, such as when they were b. and d., even if the dates are only c., and whether they liked girls or booze and what they thought of the Classical vs. the Romantic.

There are those who say, well, it doesn't make any difference if you know the author because what he writes is the real nitty-gritty gravamen of the action, and you can enjoy "The Fall of the House of Usher" without knowing that when he was eight years old somebody gave Edgar A. Poe a glass of wine and he got up and danced on the table.

This may be right, but I don't think so. Quite often when I am reading a book and there is a passage that either shakes me up or doesn't make any sense, I like to know who the author's folks are, where he went to school if at all, and maybe have a picture of him on the jacket so I can look at it and figure out whether he is the kind of person who would really intend to write that way.

Or people will say that it shouldn't be put in the papers when an author gets a divorce or wrecks his car or he is impounded for not paying his taxes or that he and his wife have four children under five years old. They say that this has nothing to do with a man's literary ability.

Yes, but I like to know these things so that when I am reading this fellow's novel I can say to myself, "This is a bad novel, but good Lord it's a wonder the poor guy can write *any* kind of a book, what with his wife's lawyers trying to get custody of the television set and the insurance company arguing about the claim and the Internal Revenue liening on his bank account and those kids yelling all day long."

I enjoy the book more knowing that the writer has all these problems. Because, after all, what right do I have to be sitting there with nothing but a manageable packet of worries and knock the work of a man who has all those crises nibbling at him?

So I would like to tell you something about myself, except what is the point of going over all that boyhood stuff about reading Tom Swift and what kind of candy you could get for a penny?

The only thing a little bit different about growing up in St. Louis was cork ball, which I have given up trying to explain to people, who don't believe it even when I do. The only foreshadowing it gave of the man I was to be is that cork ball is ideal for playing in an alley, which is what we had to play in. (By "had" I mean it was available to play in; it wasn't compulsory.)

From playing cork ball in alleys I developed into a man who can only play straight narrow games. When we played football our only plays had to be run from punt formation, right over center. An end sweep or even an off-tackle put you in somebody's ashpit or Essex roadster. With baseball we had only catcher, pitcher, second base and center field. Plus a pig-tail, of course. But nothing peripheral.

It explains why I cannot play golf which, in my experience, requires a great deal of vacant real estate in a 270-degree (at least) arc around the ball.

Another problem is that I don't remember things too well.

I have always been fascinated by those writers who can dredge up the minute details of their youth. They don't need a Proustian cupcake to transfer them back to the world of forty or fifty years ago. They remember the name of the lady who ran the notions store, their fourth-grade teacher and the golden-haired charmer who lived in the big house on the corner and played havoc with all male hearts under nine.

They are evocative of sounds, smells and colors long since past. I assume I sounded, smelled and colored as actively as they, but my recall falters.

Whenever I read these boyhood reminiscences an inner voice spoils my enjoyment by constantly nagging, "How come they can remember all the little items from 'Rosebud' on the sled and their first peek into Chapman's *Homer* on to, as the book jackets say, their awakening into awareness (and we all know what *that* means) and the day of the week on which they got their first jobs, and you can't?"

I suppose if you knew you were going to write an autobio-graphical memoir some day you would take notes from the cradle on. It never occurred to me. As a result, the only record I have of my life is in the form of daily columns which must, of necessity, be less candid than a private diary.

The reader should, therefore, be warned that in the first group of selections in this book, which is designed to tell him about the author, I cannot always be absolutely trusted in what I say about myself. There are disguises to be penetrated.

Caution in autobiography is becoming increasingly necessary, as was emphasized in the case of the actress who went to court to suppress her own book about herself. A sensitive, privacy-loving man naturally flinches at the idea of being sued for self-libel.

✳ Suggestion for an epitaph: "He went through life as unauthorized personnel."

A MAN'S HEART MAY BE IN HIS ENVIRONMENT, BUT HEREDITY IS WHERE HE GOT HIS NOSE. . . .

The changing of the calendar reminds us of the passage of time and produces a lot of writing in which people address themselves either to posterity or the past. I hesitate to speak to posterity, as they are a crowd I have never run with and I don't know whether they will be my type or not. So I thought that what I might do is drop a note of thanks to my ancestors.

I want to thank them for this big nose they gave me.

I am not a geneticist, but I know that if you want a blue-eyed fruit fly you have to be pretty particular about which fruit fly marries which. It's not just a matter of one fruit fly saying he is in love with the girl next door. You've got to check on her family and be sure that the genes and chromosomes are all blue.

Or take basketball players. They have to be planned to grow that tall.

Which is the way it is with my nose. Somewhere back in a Welsh coal pit, where the whole thing began, my ancestors had to decide whether to go in for height or noses. They opted nasally. Of course, this was long before basketball was invented and they didn't know that being 6 feet, 8 inches tall would be an advantage some day. All they knew was that it would be a pain in the neck while mining coal.

So down the centuries they have always aimed toward the Ultimate Nose. There were times when somebody might have fallen in love with a rich girl. But my ancestors never did because, apparently, the rich girls had snub noses.

The people in my family always had an instinct for the nose. They went for it, and I can only hope that the result has made them happy.

In all modesty I have to say that when someone sits down to compile a list of the Ten Great Noses of History, I will be among them. I won't rank myself, but I am right up there with Cyrano de Bergerac and Charles de Gaulle, and maybe I'm number one, because the first is fictional and the second may be also.

We don't count Jimmy Durante because he has commercialized his nose. It is a popular success and has been written up in the news magazines, which means that it is out as far as true nose connoisseurs are concerned.

As I say, when my ancestors started out on noses they had never heard of basketball any more than anybody else had, so they couldn't have known that if they had reached for height I might be 7 feet tall and have gotten my college education free. There are no scholarships for noses.

But I am far from complaining. If you are a big, tall gawk, nobody notices you. It has been drummed into everybody that tall people don't like to be asked how is the weather up there and other overworked questions. They have learned not to say to a tall person, "Pardon me if my breath is fogging your belt buckle."

The tall person is ignored because we have discovered from reading countless interviews with basketball players that they want to be treated just like anyone else. You will often see a tall person standing alone at a party. Not so the man with a really big nose.

He is surrounded by a chatty group saying witticisms such as, "Is that your nose, or are you playing the piccolo?" or,

"Well, one good thing, you can smoke a cigar in the rain."

Show me the center of hilarity and laughter, with the pretty girls and the more substantial community leaders, and I will show you a man with a big nose.

Unfortunately, some parents are so devoted to impressing upon their children that they should not comment upon physical characteristics that they overdo. They say, "Now when you meet Mr. Vaughan, whatever you do, don't comment upon the size of his nose."

I can always tell when a child has had this point hammered home. He shakes hands politely and says, "How do you do, Mr. Nose."

These parents should realize that my nose is my only claim to distinction. I like to have it mentioned, and it usually is. I don't know how millionaires feel, but I know if I were one I would be disappointed if nobody talked about my money.

Perhaps the analogy is bad. Anybody can have money. If my ancestors had gone in for money or good looks, where would I be today? Just another handsome rich man. Nobody would notice me twice. But with a nose like this they notice me three or four times.

✳ A barber I hadn't seen since I was a child recognized me the minute I climbed into the chair. "A man," he explained, "doesn't see many cowlicks like that in one lifetime."

HAIR IS FOR THE YAKS. . . .

Science has itself involved in something of a current flap over how it happened that man has turned out to be bald, in many instances, when other forms of life, such as gorillas and English sheep dogs, aren't.

I'll skip all the give-and-take on the subject and just give my view that the human species needs bald men. Apparently there is no real demand for bald gorillas or sheep dogs, so Nature, who knows what she's doing all the time, hasn't produced them.

Baldness is a tough area to think about because the minute you mention even such a relatively simple matter as a "cure" for baldness, just trying to be helpful, what happens?

What happens is that a large, angry, bald man rises up and says:

"Where do you get off talking about a cure for baldness? That is about like mentioning a cure for honesty, decency, patriotism, forthrightness and all the values that made America great.

"I want to tell you there, Curly, that what this country needs is a cure for hair."

Bald men always look angrier than anybody else, and also happier, more charming and all the rest. The reason is obvious. They have more per capita face to register their emotions over. A fellow has hair, how does the casual observer know what's going on in there among the follicles?

A man might smile with his mouth, or even twinkle with his eyes, but he could be hiding a very angry, unpleasant expression on his scalp. But not if he is bald. Then you see the whole man.

I don't know that bald men are necessarily better than the other kind, but at least they are unable to dissemble. It's all out there in the open. When you have a bald friend he is your friend clear to the back of his head, unlike those who are only your chums from the chin to the eyebrows.

There is no point in denying it. We have made fun of the bald man in our society. We have said cruel things. We will be sorry. Because the evolutionary cards are starting to run toward the bald man. A few hundred or thousand or some such brief span of years from now, almost everybody will be bald. People who have thought they were funny when they called another person Skinhead will find that the joke has swung around and if a man isn't bald there will be cries of, "Here comes old Hairhead."

What's so great about hair, anyway? According to the television commercials the girls find it excitingly disturbing, but don't you think that's a little farfetched? If you are the average American many a girl has exclaimed to you:

"I like your firm, manly handclasp."

"Those steel-gray eyes hint of hidden sadnesses."

"Your nose, Sam, is something to set a girl thinking."

We have all of us had compliments of this sort and others. But, honestly, has any lady ever told you that you have great hair?

I'm not necessarily knocking hair, but it's overrated. As leading anthropologists have pointed out, it served a purpose back in the days when Cro-Magnon would go out and the big yellow ball, as we called the sun in those days, would hit him with a shot of heat on the head. Hair was a nice insulating material.

Since then, you may have noticed, they've invented hats. Put on a hat, or sit under a beach umbrella, and you can be bald as a kumquat and still stay as cool as the hairiest kid on the block.

Try to think back, honestly. What has your hair ever done for you? Anything constructive? I doubt it. You've spent hours combing it, having it cut, washing it. As a reward it hangs in your eyes or stands up straight in back and makes you look like an idiot.

Baldness is what's happening, baby. Did I say a few hundred or thousand years? I mean a matter of weeks. Anybody who isn't bald will be trying to disguise the fact with skin wigs.

Baldness is what Mother Nature has in mind for her very favorites. Science says so, and if that weren't enough, five hairs came out in the comb this morning.

WHEN ETHNIC EYES ARE SMILIN' . . .

Every nationality, or ethnic group as we like to say around the State Department, has a grand festival day on which to indulge in those dear old songs that mist the eye and honor the heroes and ancient kings around whose heads and through whose beards many a heroic legend and bardic rune is entwined.

It is all very lonely-making for a man who has never worried too much about where the boat came from that brought the folks over.

The only solution, it seems to me, is to invent a dear old homeland of one's own.

Let us, for the sake of simplicity, call the sweet land Ethnia. It will make a bully bellow in a bar: "One Ethnic can beat any two Irishmen who ever lived."

And we'll be singing "When It's Gronch-Picking Time in Ethnia."

The leaf of the gronch, which looks very much like broccoli, is not only the Ethnic national flower but the sign by which Ethnics display their affection for the land of their forefathers. On Noodnick's Day, named after the first king of Ethnia, the gronch leaf is pinned to the shirt front and all good Ethnics exchange the traditional greeting, "Igh bas nkrm," or, "Say, isn't that a gronch leaf on your shirt front?"

To me the main charm of this idea is that it will give an opportunity for indignation. People who feel very strongly about their national background have all sorts of chances for rancor, which are denied to others with a more tenuous ancestry.

But if you choose to be an Ethnic you can have all the fun of the Italian, German, Polish or any other group.

You can denounce politicians: "He'll get the Ethnic vote

on the day gronches sprout strawberries. What has he ever done for Ethnia?"

You can write angry letters to magazines: "In your recent issue devoted to world travel, it was extremely disappointing that no mention was made of Ethnia, with its many attractions. Why do you not send one of your so-called editors to Scuf, the lovely old capital city, and get a real write-up of the Noodnick's Day Gronchfest? On second thought it won't do you any good because I am canceling my subscription and all my Ethnic friends are doing the same. 'Nak tvy ossam' to you and yours, as King Noodnick said when he put the curse on the gronch weevil."

Or you can be just generally belligerent: "Whadda ya mean Sophia Loren? Listen, the prettiest girls in the world are Ethnic. From the Valley of the Yut. Listen, my mother was an Ethnic girl. You makin' cracks about my mother or something there, Mac?"

And so it will go. A whole wide, wonderful world will open up, as soon as we get a few details worked out. And we've really got to get busy on picking out a Noodnick's Day date in time for the Governor to proclaim it and decorate Main Street with gronch branches.

"Nk var agootay?"

✳ An aspiring folk singer admits, with some embarrassment, that he is only Ethnic on his mother's side.

THE LAST OF THE RED HOT TAX-WORRIERS . . .

Early April is when I absent myself from felicity to tell my story to the Internal Revenue Service. Which, I hasten to assure everybody, I don't mind doing. After all, we have to buy all that vomit gas and dams and paper clips, don't we?

But what frightens me, and at the same time makes me feel that I should be memorialized in some way, is that I seem to be alone.

When someone notices my general seedy appearance in April and I explain that it is because of the, you know, income tax, they don't even know what I am talking about.

"Why," they will say, "I have this wonderful little tax man and he works it all out and gives me the result in a leather folder with my gold-leaf initials on the front."

Nobody has a big tax man. It's always "my little tax man." Word about them doesn't help me at all. It even makes me have dreams about little tax men, all in green with peaked caps. I wish I had one. (A little tax man, not a peaked cap.)

If I say to some such friends, "But I don't have a little tax man," they say, "You don't need one. Just read the instructions."

I read the instructions. I don't see any place where it says you don't have to sit around drinking black coffee, stubbing out cigarettes, yelling at your children and kicking wastebaskets. Maybe they get different instructions than I do. All it ever says in the instructions I get is "Send the money."

Other people did their income tax returns months ago. In January. Can you imagine anybody doing a tax return in January? Apparently you can because that's when so many of you do your tax return.

I wait until April because I keep hoping that at least the weather will be better. I mean, when you're sitting there biting pencils it's nice to look out and see that there is sunshine and an occasional crocus.

All this, of course, makes me a terrible anachronism, which is why I think some foundation should support me as a bit of vanishing Americana.

Especially since, as I understand it, foundation grants are nontaxable.

THAT'S THE SINCERITY KEY RIGHT NEXT TO THE
MARGIN RELEASE. . . .

Somebody says an unkind word about the dog or the cat and
powerful interests rise up to smite him. Almost everything is
protected and hedged about with anti-defamation commit-
tees. There is a National Pencil Week, and if you knock the
pencil during the period of its observance you are condemned, maybe for life, to trying to write with a 4H pencil
on slick paper.

But one of my best friends, dearer to me than dog, cat or
pencil, gets slandered and put down, and only this lonesome
voice is raised in its defense. I refer to the typewriter.

I was talking a little while ago to Philip Dunne, the Hollywood scenario writer and son of Finley Peter Dunne, creator
of the immortal Mister Dooley. Dunne said that he always
wrote in longhand and quoted his father as referring to the
typewriter as "the assassin of style."

Then, in *Dorothy and Red,* an account of the marriage of
Dorothy Thompson and Sinclair Lewis, Vincent Sheean ap-
pends this comment to one of Miss Thompson's poignant letters:

"On the whole, the foregoing letter is an outpouring of sincere emotion, even though written on the typewriter."

It should be noted that these expressions of contumely do
not come from some lunatic fringe Back-to-the-Goosequill
radicals, but from reliable, indeed gifted, men. Nor is there
any suspicion that either is a large holder of stock in fountain
pen or ink companies.

When men of the status of Philip Dunne and Vincent
Sheean attack the typewriter they must be taken seriously.
We must try to understand their viewpoint. It may be that
they have had unpleasant experiences with typewriters. This

can happen. Not all typewriters are perfect, any more than all dogs, cats, pencils or people.

I once owned a portable which had very small keys. For a man who operates as I do out of a pouncing position, which involves coming down on the keyboard from a considerable height, they presented an unsatisfactory target. As a consequence the finger often went between the keys. On a piano, the black keys are put there to prevent just such a thing happening. But on typewriters, this particular one anyway, there was nothing but space. Only enough space, however, to permit the finger to pass between the keys; not enough to allow it to be extracted.

The portable was very light (that was its sole lovable characteristic), and when an attempt was made to withdraw the finger the typewriter came right along with it and had to be shaken off, in the manner of a dog getting rid of a mousetrap on its paw.

But I don't judge all typewriters by the one bad one I have met. As far as the outpouring of sincere emotion is concerned, I rate the typewriter way up ahead of any other writing instrument. If you want to express anger or bitterness, you can slam at it with great sledgehammer blows. For the light touch, you naturally type lightly, with lots of wrist motion. A man can type from a crouch, or sitting severely erect; he can pound or peck, depending on his mood.

I am not speaking, of course, of the touch-typist, a new breed which puts speed and neatness ahead of personality. I would hate to have any typewriter I have loved, lived and quarreled with subjected to the monotony of the touch-typist.

Far from being the assassin of style, the good typewriter is a constant source of helpfulness. Just a few days ago I was typing a letter which involved the word "ultimately." The typewriter changed it to "umtilately," a far better and more expressive word, and one which would never have occurred to a pen or pencil.

The typewriter lends itself to any kind of writing, while other tools actually dictate the style. If you are writing a note with a blunt, black pencil you will start it out, "Hi, Hon," whereas with a fine penpoint you will begin, "My beloved Delphine." If there's green ink in it, you are not only led to further extravagances but find yourself dotting the *i*'s with little circles.

On the whole, the foregoing is an outpouring of sincere emotion.

TYPO-SPEAK: NOTES FOR A UNIVERSAL LANGUAGE . . .

On one of those rare occasions when I tamper with the breakfast cooking, I put the fried egg in front of the assembled gourmets and say: "Viola!"

This is an example of what I think of as typo-talk. Ever since I came West with a shirttail full of type to establish journalism on the frontier, I have lived and grown with the typographical error.

I have now reached a point where I find it simpler to put the typo right in the talk rather than wait for it to appear in print.

Having been to a heavily endowed university, I know that there is a French word that calls itself "Voilà." In the lexicon of most Americans and 97 per cent of the nation's loyal linotype machines, it comes out "Viola."

So why not say: "Viola," and get rid of embarrassment?

"Viola," as a matter of fact, is a better word than Voilà, which lends itself to being pronounced wrong. I have outgrown that kind of thing, but if you have the girl in the candlelit nook with Flamingo records on the hi-fi, and you produce a bottle of champagne, it is dangerous to say "Voilà."

She may fault your pronunciation. Or, frightened by the

sheer Frenchiness, she may remember that the last bus leaves at 10:30.

It is much better to say "Viola," a word which can't be mispronounced and will, as well, give her a feeling of trust in your all-American boyishness.

Eagle eyes may have spotted a couple of paragraphs upstream where I said Flamingo records. I tossed it in as an example of typo-talk. Flamenco is the whatever, and flamingo is the bird. I know that as well as you do, but there's no chance of smuggling it past a proofreader.

For a while I dedicated myself to getting the Scottish sport of caber-tossing into my perceptive dispatches. It always came out "sabre." Many a writer goes to an untimely grave worrying about this sort of thing.

What they should do is adopt typo-talk and call it sabre-tossing in the first place.

"I would invite you home for dinner tonight, old pal," I will tell an old pal, "but we are having a great deal of martial discord at my place."

Experience has taught me that there is no chance at all of getting marital and martial straightened out in print, so why not call it "martial discord" right off and avoid the worry?

People have been known to look askance at me when I say, "Some day I dream of deserting the rat race and finding my own Shangri, Louisiana." They think it should be Shangri La, and so do I, but in typo-talk, with the errors built in, it has to be Shangri, Louisiana.

MAKE EVERY HOLIDAY A FESTIVAL OF WORK . . .

"To what," the young supplicant asked of the good, gray, columnist, "do you owe not only your vast age but the serene wisdom with which you face the closing years?"

"Sam," he said, "if that is your name (parenthetically I knew your Dad), the great secret is that I selected an occupation which permitted me to work on holidays. Permitted, did I say? Nay, often insisted."

"But," said the young supplicant, "holidays are for restoring the soul and refreshing the body. If they didn't do stuff like that why would they be written into the union contracts?"

"That is not for me to say," said the good, gray columnist. "All I know is that men with whom I started out in the race of life are faltering and dropping by the wayside. They are breaking stride, gasping for breath and retiring to the golf course.

"I have to ask myself the reason. I am not endowed with an unusually robust constitution. I keep clean living within reasonable bounds. So why do I thrive while they, brave and gallant souls, wither?

"The only answer I can come up with is that they have had the misfortune to have careers of the type which permit, encourage, or even require them to take holidays off.

"Let us take, as an example, the Fourth of July. For forty Fourths of July they have been at home, with the dog cowering under the sofa, the firecrackers popping and the neighbors dropping in to borrow a tray of ice and staying for two days. Or they have been at the lake, blistering, falling overboard, sleeping in tents. Or on the highway, yelling, 'O.K., you kids in the back seat, shut up,' and watching the wristwatch and speedometer to be sure that they're not falling behind the requisite sixty-five miles an hour average.

"Wearing on a man. Very wearing.

"I, on the other hand, have spent those same forty Fourths of July calmly at the office, going about my accustomed tasks. Patriotic as the next man, I look out the window at the flags flaunted in the breeze and think of the forefathers who established this great country of ours.

"Working on the Fourth of July gives a man time to be patriotic. If he is out in the park, angrily battling for possession of a picnic table, he has virtually no opportunity to turn his thoughts to Valley Forge or the rude bridge that spanned the flood.

"Not that I have cut myself off from my family entirely on these occasions. From time to time the phone will ring and I will say such things as:

" 'Take her to the hospital.'

" 'Take him to the vet's.'

" 'Try a cube of ice at the back of the neck.'

" 'Call the fire department.'

"Crises happen even in those happy homes where the father works on holidays. But observe how much more help it was to have me at the office, from where I could issue calm, sensible directions, rather than being at home, getting in the way.

"George Washington didn't take his birthday off work and neither did Abraham Lincoln. Frankly it makes me feel closer to them when I observe their birthdays the same way they did.

"I hear a lot of things about Christmas—broken toys and whining children and frayed tempers. They make me sorry for family men who have to stay at home on Christmas and have their illusions destroyed. Since I am never there, I think of Christmas in terms of happiness and warmth, with rosy-cheeked children dancing in gratitude around their simple presents.

"Another thing, working on holidays gives a man a wonderful feeling of sacrifice, bordering on martyrdom. It also gives him plenty of parking places to choose from.

"Try a simple test. Look around any gathering and the oldest, weariest looking men there are likely to be the ones who are in jobs where they take all the holidays.

"Understand, I don't want to abolish holidays. The more

the better, in fact. Because if there weren't holidays there wouldn't be any advantage in working on them."

THE SKY IS FRIENDLY, IF YOU CAN EVER GET INTO IT. . . .

Whatever we may think of the ethics of the sixteen-year-old who flew from Kansas City to London without a ticket, apparently by picking the right flights and flashing an empty loading envelope, we must be impressed by the aplomb of the generation he represents.

It is a quality which I, at least, excessively lack. Getting on an airplane is an ordeal.

In the first place, I am obsessed with the idea that I am about to miss my flight. Sitting in the coffee shop, an hour before the scheduled departure, I see a sign on the wall: "No Flight Announcements." It has the same effect on me as though it said "Cholera." I gulp my coffee and rush outside where I can hear the loudspeaker, which I never understand.

It says, "Passenger Wahh W. Wahh for Wahhwahh, please come to the Wahh Wahh Airline ticket counter. Passenger Wahh."

I rush up to the nearest uniformed figure and surrender:

"What did I do wrong? I'm sorry. If there's anything extra I'll pay."

It turns out, of course, that it is not my airline or my destination and that the man they want is indeed a Passenger Wahh. I have never, incidentally, seen any of the Passengers Wahh, but they are a family that travels extensively. At least they always seem to be going somewhere on days when I am in an air terminal.

Even more chilling is when the horn says, "Wahhwahh Airlines announces the departure of its Slippery Elm Green Carpet Flight Wahh to Wahh. Leaving from Gate 9, Concourse G, Finger 112. All passengers please board."

Great Scott!

It doesn't sound like my flight, but it's leaving, while I'm standing here buying a newspaper. I don't dare take a chance. Gate 9, Concourse G, Finger 112 is so far away it's in a different time zone, so I gain an hour but I would have missed the plane even if it had been mine which, I discover, when I get there, it isn't.

Most air passengers only check in at the ticket counter once. I do it two or three times. How do I know that the last fellow who checked me in was really a ticket person? Anybody can fake a uniform. Maybe he was a sixteen-year-old boy trying to get to London.

I go back for reassurance. They get so they remember me and say that they don't have to check my ticket again. I beg them to do it anyway. The last man who stamped it was using a wornout ink pad. Suppose I get thrown off the plane because the stamp is illegible? They say there is really nothing more they need to do. I invite them to get my luggage back and weigh it again. They say it won't be necessary.

When the time comes to board the plane, I check in at the gate. The man says, "Thank you, sir," and I say, "Does this plane go to Chicago?" He says, "No, why?" and I say, "Well, so many of them do. Go to Chicago that is, and I'm not. I'm going to Los Angeles to see my sister's oldest boy who's in the hardware game."

He says this plane is going to Los Angeles, but I check it again at the foot of the gangplank with a man who has mufflers on his ears. I yell, "Los Angeles?" at him and he nods. At the top of the stairs I show my ticket to the stewardess and explain to her about the wornout rubber stamp. It's pretty noisy but she nods and says, "Wahh."

What does she mean by that? It worries me. I go up and

down the aisle asking everybody if they are going to Chicago. They all say they aren't, which reassures me. But after I've asked them if they're going to Chicago they all take their tickets out and look at them again, which starts me worrying all over.

Well, of course, I get to Los Angeles all right. But it just proves one of the handicaps of being born before the age of air.

That kid stowed away easier than I can fly with a paid-up ticket.

THE HUMIDITY/STUPIDITY INDEX . . .

Friends, I know that there are worse problems in the world. I read the papers. But it's hard to concentrate on the big worries when you have a small one going for you at the same time.

The thing that happens is that you carry an umbrella to work on a rainy morning and when you leave that afternoon the weather has cleared and you walk off and forget the umbrella.

The next day your wife says, threateningly, "Don't forget the umbrella, Sam."

It is a bright day, full of sunshine and heat shimmering off the asphalt. That afternoon you have the problem of carrying the umbrella home on the bus without looking like some species of filbert.

Bus stop humorists are unable to resist the sight of a man carrying an umbrella when the nearest rain cloud is hovering over Intermittent, N.D.

"Well, Mr. Chamberlain," they will say, "does it look like peace in our time?"

If it's a raincoat you are involved with you can wrap it up and stick it in a paper sack or some such. But how are you going to wrap an umbrella so it looks like anything but an umbrella?

You can, of course, sit as far away from the umbrella as you can and pretend that it doesn't belong to you. But this can be tricky.

I tried it one time and an acquaintance sat down next to me and said, "Is that your umbrella?"

"Why, uh, no," I said. "I just found it."

And he said, "Oh," rather suspiciously, so when I got to the stop near my house I had to take the umbrella and, because the acquaintance was watching me (a fellow I never really liked), I had to turn it in to the bus driver and tell him that I seemed to have found this umbrella.

Then, the next morning, I had to call the lost-and-found department of the bus company and ask them if anybody had found my umbrella.

"No, sir," the man said after he had gone away from the phone for a while to see about it. "We got a left shoe and a trombone but no umbrella."

"I happen to know better," I said. "My umbrella was found yesterday on bus No. 18975 and turned in to the driver."

"How come you're so sure?"

"Because I found it myself."

Click!

A half hour later I had my wife call and by this time they had found the umbrella and asked her to describe it, which she did.

"When did you say your husband lost the umbrella?" the man asked her.

"Yesterday."

"What was your husband doing carrying an umbrella yesterday?" the man wanted to know. "The sun shone all day."

"Because he is a nut," said my wife.

"Is he the same one who called a while ago and said he found his own umbrella and gave it to the driver?"

"I'm afraid so," said my wife.

"You poor thing," said the man.

I finally got the umbrella back. But not that day because it was raining too hard to go to the lost-and-found place. I had to wait until the next day, when the sun was shining.

I got it home by running it down one leg of my pants, with the handle hooked over my belt. There were only a few people on the bus but I had to stand up all the way home because of the umbrella in my pants leg.

The same acquaintance got on and asked why I didn't sit down next to him and I told him, "No, sir, I got in enough trouble sitting next to you a couple of days ago."

He went and sat behind the driver, and when I got off I'm pretty sure I heard one of them say to the other, "That nut looks like he's got an umbrella in there somewhere."

ARE THE PUSH BUTTONS BEGINNING TO PUSH BACK?

I have been handed a letter which purports to come from someone signing himself A. Faithful Servant, Your Automobile. It starts out mawkishly by addressing me as Dear Boss, and goes on to say, "I notice you are wearing a jacket this morning. It's a little chilly, isn't it? As you prepare yourself for cold weather, don't forget about me!"

That gives you an idea of the general tone of this communication, which whines on for about seven paragraphs of self-pity, mixed with demands for antifreeze and winter weight oil and a new battery and other costly luxuries.

Not only is it a new high in insincerity for an automobile

to address its owner as "Boss," but A. Faithful Servant compounds its egregiousness by subscribing itself, "Sincerely yours."

It's just about what I would expect from this particular car which has been a surly troublemaker, garage lawyer and gasoline gourmand in all the years of our acquaintance. As far as its letter is concerned I considered the source and disregarded it.

But I hope that this isn't the beginning of a trend. In spite of his best intentions and the fervent promises he made to himself in his youth, a man does accumulate a certain amount of household goods as he goes along, and I'd hate it if they all started writing me letters.

The stomach tenses as we picture the scene at the breakfast table.

"Anything in the mail this morning, my dear?" I would ask. (It's a sign of real class to eat breakfast so late that the mail has already arrived.)

"Just bills and ads and, oh yes, this note from the icebox."

The icebox and I have always gotten along pretty well, and I could not help but be chilled by the icy formality of its missive:

"Dear Fatso: I notice you aren't able to button your bathrobe any more. This came to my attention when you woke me up at 1 o'clock this morning to go poking around in my insides for a leftover wedge of chocolate pie. Your lack of consideration in rousing me for these 'snacks' of yours has been giving me a pain in the coils for a long time now, but I have not felt it my place to complain. After all, you are the Boss; we machines are the humble servants. But the fact that they are not only ruining my repose but your figure as well has led me to take this step. If you do not initiate immediate remedial action I shall have no recourse save to padlock myself. Yours sincerely, A. Refrigerator."

"Why, that ungrateful tin box," I would snarl. "After all the times I have defrosted it. Any more of its lip and I'll unscrew its little light bulb."

Another morning it might be a complaint from the television set:

"Dear Clod: Well, you did it again. If you think it's easy for me to sit here bringing you songs, dances, funny stories, heartrending dramas, spies, Indians and weather charts, you've got another think coming. Not that I mind so much, that's Show Biz and what I'm here for. But, believe me, it's discouraging when I look out and all I see is you sound asleep in that crummy chair of yours, or maybe even reading a book. How do you think that makes a performer feel? Worst of all, last night you even went to bed and left me turned on. Any more of that stuff and I'm going to flip my vertical hold in the last three minutes of a tie football game and drive you crazy. Yours sincerely, A. Teevy."

I'll tell you, the kind of mail I get now is dismal enough without hearing from all the appliances. Not, anyway, if they're going to all take that hangdog, long-suffering tone which characterizes the letter from A. Faithful Servant. Of course, it would be all right if some of them would write encouraging, even complimentary, notes, such as:

"It was a pleasure to play for your dancing enjoyment last night. You are a regular Pat Rooney. Yours admiringly, A. Hi-Fi." or "You will never know how complimented I was when you put on my shade as a hat. It was the high point of the evening. Yours lovingly, A. Floor Lamp."

But that would be too much to expect and, on balance, I think it would be better if the inanimate objects around the house kept their opinions to themselves. And some of the animate ones, too.

TURN YOUR HOBBY INTO INSTANT POVERTY. . . .

When I feel the need of having my heart warmed I find nothing does it quite as well as reading one of those success stories about how some nice little family starts bottling Aunt Nora's salad dressing and first thing you know they've got a fleet of trucks delivering the stuff and a cable address, like maybe Antnor.

We all know of cases like this. Perhaps we have had a neighbor who has hacked around all his life without accomplishing much except that there is one thing he learned to do as a boy which was to staple pieces of flannel together to make a handy penwiper and he adds a certain touch by covering the staple with an acorn or a pine cone. For years he has been giving them to people for birthday, anniversary and Christmas presents or to bear a "Get Well" message.

Naturally, like all the neighbors, we have a number of these penwipers around the house and a visiting capitalist spots one and cries: "Why, wherever did you get this?"

And you tell him that it is sort of a hobby with Sam down the block and he dashes off to Sam's house with a checkbook and a fountain pen. The next you hear is that they're tooling up a factory in New Jersey, a multimillion-dollar advertising campaign has been launched, subcontractors are supplying plastic acorns and pine cones and the stock is listed on the big board.

Heaven forbid that any of us would be so narrow as to envy any friend, neighbor or name in the newspaper this sudden accesssion of commercial grandeur. And yet I must admit to a certain pique that nothing of this sort ever happens to me.

More than once I have sampled a forkful of something delicious at the family table and shouted, "Great Scott, Hortense, these hominy grits popovers with sauce béarnaise are a culinary triumph! Where is the treasured old family receipt with which we will get rolling, starting first in a small way in our own folksy kitchen, you with an endearing smudge of flour on your tip-tilted nose and me and the boys delivering the product in the old family sedan—call the photographers—and by next year we'll be in our own spotless 15-acre plant but still giving each popover the treasured old family attention and loving care?"

"Sorry, love," says Hortense, "but these popovers were personally popped over by kindly Mrs. Kroger who has the supermarket on the corner. She has two shelves full of them."

Not only does this dash the spirits, but I don't care if I never eat another hominy grits popover with or without sauce béarnaise.

Nor does there seem to be much hope that I will ever whomp up something in my basement workshop that will fill a vast need. One reason may be that I don't have a basement workshop.

There is no point in my thinking that I will produce a wren house that would tempt foreign investors to promote me into an international corporation.

In the olden times I took a class in manual training, where the first thing to make was a breadboard. A breadboard is, basically, a piece of plank which was what you started out with. But it had to be level. Who knows why? I have sliced my share of bread, and I never saw that an eighth of an inch deviation on the cutting surface made much difference, especially considering the way I slice bread. The instructor was very firm about it, however, and I kept running out of wood after planing down one side to match the other. While other little boys of the era were making Uncle Sam mailbox holders and tabourets (What ever happened to tabourets?) I was coming back for another piece of wood to destroy in the vain dream of making a breadboard.

Anyway, even if I could make a great breadboard, who slices bread any more? (Although, for that matter, who wipes pens, and look how well the guy did with the penwipers.)

I still have hopes of wealth beyond the dreams of avarice, but apparently it isn't going to come out of anything that any member of the family is producing. We're going to have to strike oil in the window box or something along those lines.

WHY, I BELIEVE IT'S A RUBY-THROATED TRANQUILIZER . . .

One of the great things about getting out where Nature has not been trammeled is that you can observe the birds. Two or more people can sit amid the trees, power poles and fence posts of the forest primeval, and if they concentrate on the birds, they will find themselves in peaceful communion with one another, with all the bitterness, hatred and pressures of the workaday world only a dim and unpleasant memory.

I was in such a mood the other day as I sat, overlooking an Ozarks lake, while smoking an afternoon pipe, with the stem of which, having removed it from my mouth, I pointed and remarked to a friend who is a highly touted amateur of ornithology, "That little long-tailed, small-headed bird which is perched upon the clothesline, what sort of a rare species would you take him to be?"

"Where do you see this bird," he asked, "which sounds like either a long-tailed nithead or a nit-headed longtail, two separate birds, although often mistaken for each other."

"Just over the peak of the well-house there," I said, "between the red bathing suit and the dish towel."

He consulted the library of Audobon and other authorities on the birds which he keeps constantly at his elbow, then trained his binoculars on the bird. I rate bird-watchers by the size of their binoculars and this man is a very big binocular indeed.

He looked at it carefully, riffled some pages in his guidebooks, gazed again, put down the binoculars, sighed and said, "That is a clothespin."

"Really," I said. "I had no idea they migrated this far north."

"They don't migrate," he said.

"Then," I asked, "how did it get on your clothesline?"

"My wife put it there," he said. "It is a common wooden clothespin."

"Not a rare bird then?"

"Not even a bird, old friend," he said patiently. "Just a clothespin, as any knucklehead could have plainly seen."

A silence fell as I told myself how pleasant it was to be engaged in this peaceful discussion of the beauties of Nature, far from the marts of trade where men argue, bicker and fight over pieces of paper and coins of what used to be silver.

"Old friend," I said at last, "if you will look over there between the red bathing suit and the dish towel, you will see that your clothespin has just flown away."

"Oh," he said. "That was a lesser tufted potlatch. I thought you meant that clothespin by the blue bathing suit."

"Are you color-blind?" I asked.

"You mean to imply," he retorted, "that a man who has made a career of distinguishing among birds by such matters as whether their breast is a greenish-yellow shading into a tawny umber, is color-blind?"

"You can't tell a red bathing suit from a blue bathing suit," I said.

"You can't tell a clothespin from a tufted potlatch," he snapped.

"I can now," I replied with some acerbity. "One of them can fly."

His face flushed and he bit angrily at his lip.

"I just saw a raspy-throated finch," he cried. "And you didn't."

"What makes you think I didn't see him?" I said.

"Because," he said, "birds hate to be watched by ignoramuses who voted for Lyndon Johnson and think that clothespins can fly."

"You may not like my politics," I said, "but at least I don't go around making stupid remarks about Vietnam. Lend me your binoculars."

"I won't," he said, "you'll break them like you broke my camera."

"That was in 1957."

"You see," he said triumphantly, "every ten years you break something of mine. Anyway I don't want an idiot who doesn't know anything about birds watching my birds, and what's so stupid about my remarks about Vietnam?"

So I told him and he went into the cabin and slammed the door, and I'm afraid we may have to reconsider our thinking on the peace-making qualities of a shared love of Nature.

(NOTE: The names of all birds mentioned have been changed to protect the innocent. Except for the clothespin.)

NOSTALGIA, THE TARNISH ON THE GOLDEN YEARS . . .

I wasn't really too surprised when the mail brought a lovely brochure from a retirement village, or whatever the generic term is for those settlements where you go to live out the sunset years. After all, thanks to the wonders of modern medical science, we are getting old younger than ever before.

Still, I don't think I will move to any of the sun-drenched communities so glowingly described in the literature. They are tempting, of course. All we neat old men with our ruddy complexions and trim figures may be seen in four-color photographs, cooking steaks on outdoor grills, playing golf, indulging in arts and crafts, even managing to look not too unattractive in swimming trunks.

Our retired wives are even neater and trimmer than we are, and their hair is varying shades of blue.

With a future like this beckoning to him, a man can hardly wait to get old. Except . . .

Except that the copywriter, carried away by his enthusiasm, tells us how friendly it is all going to be when we Senior Citizens foregather without any young folks around. He says that we will be there together, all of us:

"People who watched John Barrymore and Ann Harding, listened to Caruso, remember going to the airport just to watch the planes, whose eyes will twinkle at the mention of rumble seats and roadsters, who met the challenge of the Depression, helped win our nation's wars, and have had a part in the work and achievements which have given America her greatest era."

I tell you, friends, this all sounds perfectly fine, but my goal in life at the moment is to escape from nostalgia. We are drowning in nostalgia like it was caramel sauce. You can't pick up a mass medium without reading about Ann Harding or the rumble seat.

I am always glad to see Ann Harding on the Late, Late, but I don't want to sit around in some geriatric paradise listening to somebody say, "Hey, Sam, do you remember Ann Harding?" I have my memories of Ann Harding and why should I share them with a retired dentist from Sheboygan any more than he should share his with me?

The rumble seat as a conversational gambit also seems to me to have its limits.

After you have asked the contractor, out to pasture from Cleveland, if he remembers rumble seats and he has twinkled his eyes at you, what's left? Here you are with a lifetime contract and—for all I know—a high wall around the place and you've run out of things to talk about.

Certainly nobody who met the challenge of the Depression and helped win our nation's wars—whatever that means; that we survived these interesting events, I suppose—is going to bring them up. To do so is to risk getting talked to death before your time.

No, gentlemen, before I commit myself to one of these projects I want to make it clear: The climate is optional. I don't need golf courses, swimming pools or pottery kilns; I just want to be sure of one thing: Are the premises 100 per cent free of nostalgia?

WITH A MUSE LIKE THIS, WHAT'S AN AUTHOR TO DO?

I had a midnight visit recently from my Muse, a large and roseate lady who smokes cigars. I wish she wouldn't make these calls at unconventional hours. It causes talk among the neighbors, what with the chariot parked in front of the house and all. Still, she is one of the few Muses that make house calls any more. It sort of restores your faith in the profession.

As we know from reading the ancient poets, Muses were always rapping on their chamber doors with inspiration. Nowadays when you see a poet he is hurrying to the classroom or the library, which is where the Muses have their office hours. You have to go to them. Thursday is their day off.

I suppose this is one reason I stick with this particular Muse. Anyway, she perched on the side of the bed. Thank goodness nobody else woke up. You know how loosely wrapped Muses are. A perfectly respectable class of girl but always giving the impression that they are about to fall out of their clothes.

Explanations can be difficult: "Dear, I believe you know my Muse."

Chilly glances are exchanged.

This is apart from the subject. A writer can't operate without a Muse, and if there are misunderstandings, why it's all in the game.

The big trouble with this Muse, though, is that she has such punk ideas. Do you know what she woke me up for?

She said, "Sam, I'll bet you will write something about National Pickle Week."

And I said, "I'll bet I won't."

"There are possibilities," she said, relighting her cigar. "You can make fun of it, for example. You can say that it is ridiculous. I mean, stacked up against Brotherhood Week or Mental Health Week, Pickle Week seems pretty frivolous."

"I don't know about that," I said. "Year-round I see more pickles than I do Brotherhood or Mental Health. Measured by results alone, it seems to me that Pickle Week does a better job of pushing the product than Brotherhood or Mental Health weeks."

"See," said my Muse. "I knew you could write something about Pickle Week. You came up with the angle, Sam baby."

"No," I said. "I'm not going to write that Pickle Week is better than Brotherhood Week or Mental Health Week because I believe in Brotherhood and Mental Health more than I do pickles."

"Say," she said, "you might do a combination piece on Brotherhood and Pickles. It would be a catchy slogan: 'Take a Pickle to Lunch.'

"Do you know what the theme of National Pickle Week is this year?" my Muse went on.

"No, and I don't want to."

"Traffic safety," she said. "They have a bumper sticker alerting the people that for maximum safety they should drive 150 pickle lengths behind the car ahead."

"What sort of pickles," I asked, slightly interested, "gherkin, dill or watermelon?"

"Aha," she said, "you are slightly interested. That's good. The kind of pickle doesn't matter. The point is that it's in the cause of traffic safety, which is at least as important as Brotherhood and Mental Health."

"I'll take care of it during Traffic Safety Week," I said.

"People," she said, "will think you are anti-safety."

"The president of the high-level Business Council," I pointed out, "says that safety is a fad, like the hula hoop."

"There's the angle, Sam baby," said my Muse. "Get it down on paper that safety is a sometime thing, but pickles are forever."

"I won't," I said. "I won't write a thing about National Pickle Week."

And my Muse smiled.

"Want to bet, Sam baby?" she murmured drawing her draperies around her and departing, leaving only a faint aroma of cigars to be, somehow, explained.

The publishers of this book have a thing they sometimes do with their novels of detection and espionage. When the suspense becomes, theoretically, unbearable, the rest of the pages are sealed. If the reader can quit without finding out what happens, he can take the book back to the store and the nice lady will cheerfully refund his money.

My thought was that right here, after you have read these opening essays of a personal nature, we would put a seal. Then, if you decided I wasn't the sort of person you wanted to be associated with in a literary manner, you could turn in the book and get your money back.

There were some pretty funny interoffice memos about it.

✳✳✳✳

THE SOLID MAHOGANY
BOOBY-TRAP

Or: Work as an occupational hazard

✳✳✳✳

The way things are shaping up for most Americans, or at least this is the dream, is that we spend one third of our lives getting an education and another third enjoying the Golden Years of retirement. A mathematical check indicates that this leaves yet another third of our life span between mortarboard and shuffleboard which is just plain bored.

These are the years that we spend in productive endeavor. That means work, you idiot. It comes to us highly recommended by eminent authorities. And besides there isn't much of any way to get out of it.

I don't know what your job is, but I can tell you a few things about it. For example, you do more than your fair share of the work because everybody else in the place is either some fresh kid who thinks he knows it all and has no respect for experience and is always thinking about girls or hot rods and maybe worse, or they are dead wood who are just cluttering up the place waiting for their pension. This leaves only you to shoulder the load, but nobody appreciates it and you are underpaid. At least I have never heard you complain about being overpaid.

And you started out at the bottom of the ladder. You learned the business from the ground up, and nobody coddled you or willed you any big money. Because you go about your work with cheerful competence you have been passed over for promotion by people who are always griping and stealing your ideas.

It's the squeaky wheel that gets the grease, am I right?

If you'd had just a few breaks and a little capital to take advantage of an opportunity or two that came your way you'd be somewhere on your yacht right now instead of eating a peanut butter sandwich out of a paper sack.

I may be wrong on a few details, but isn't that a basically accurate description of your career?

And isn't it funny that your job, whatever it may be, should sound almost exactly like mine?

WHATEVER HAPPENED TO THOSE GOOD, OLD CAREFREE DAYS?

I was bustling through the checkout stand at the supermarket the other day when the lady on duty there said to me, "I care about you."

I told her that was nice but I was double-parked, and she said that I had misinterpreted her meaning.

"Personally," she said, "I don't care. I couldn't care less. To me you are just $8.97 worth of poorly selected groceries and a string of savings stamps, but it's our corporate policy. We care about you. The company cares."

"That's nice," I said. "How about taking a check for this?"

"We just care," she said, "we don't cash."

I fished around and came up with the money and went on my way with a warm feeling. It is nice to have somebody care, but it started me to noticing, and I discovered that there is more caring going on in our society right now than I care to think about.

In addition to supermarkets, there are gasoline stations that care. They say so in their advertising.

I drove into one and the man said, "So?"

I said I didn't want any gasoline or oil, but I hated to drive past when he cared so much. He wanted to know if I were some kind of wise guy and I said no, or only in the sense that wisdom is a form of caring. What kind of man would see a filling station operated by an oil company that cared about him and drive uncaringly by? I told the man that I had stopped to let him know that I cared that his company cared.

He informed me that I was parked on the rubber hose that dings the little bell inside the station. I asked if this meant that he didn't care. He said it meant that he cared about that bell dinging and my holding up customers who would like to buy some gasoline. He said he cared very deeply about that.

Once a man is awakened to the fact that everybody around him cares it changes his life. It brings new responsibilities. I have a bank that puts a little slip into my monthly statement telling me that it is "The Bank That Cares."

How can you overdraw your account with a bank that cares? I thought for a while of taking my money out and putting it into the Bank That Doesn't Pay Attention, but even if I could find that kind of a bank, my conscience wouldn't let me sleep nights.

Because when somebody cares about you, why you have a duty not to let them down. Most of us grew up being as generally nice as we are because somebody cared.

Being cared about is a beautiful thing, but it can be kind of smothering. Take a man who is about to cheat on his golf score. He looks up and there is a billboard which says, "The Crankshaft Laundry Cares About Your Shirts." Well, my gosh, if a laundry where you don't even do business cares about your shirts it would be pretty shoddy of you not to count all the strokes it took you to get out of the sand trap.

An insurance salesman came into the office the other day and said I should take out a policy with him because his company cares about me.

I gave him a regretful no.

"I care about your company, Sam," I told him, "and I care that they care about me. The trouble is that if I bought into the action it might rend the fabric of this beautiful mutual caring. In spite of myself, I would be thinking unworthy thoughts, such as, 'Does Inevitable Life really care about me for myself alone or does it care because I am an insured risk?'

"The way it is now I can feel that your people back there in Hartford or wherever care about whether I smoke too much just because, well, just because they care. But if it was going to be to their financial advantage to keep me healthy, I think you can see that I could never be certain about the basis for their concern."

He said he understood perfectly and assured me that he and his company still cared and I said me, too.

It makes for a rather long day from the breakfast muffin prepared by the Bakers Who Care to the evening when a man finally sinks into the Mattress That Cares. All presided over, of course, by the watchful eye in Washington of the President Who Cares.

This careful nurture through the day by People Who Care can be emotionally exhausting, and a man can't be blamed if he occasionally rebels by shutting doors and windows, pulling the shades and putting on the hi-fi his old record of Eva Tanguay singing, "I Don't Care."

WHAT KIND OF BREAKFAST IS BACON AND RHETORIC?

Dawn comes to the city. The slumbering giant awakens. Lights come on. The milkman clinks his bottles. It is an old and familiar picture, but something new has been added. In hotels, cafeterias and restaurants of all kinds, what are people doing? They are making speeches.

It is a thought which would have chilled our ancestors and will, I devoutly hope, seem strange to our descendants. But for this generation the Breakfast Meeting has become a reality.

At unearthly hours such as 8 A.M., rational, or at least neatly dressed, men are listening to talks on "Personnel Practices at the Crossroads," "The Challenge of Automation" and "The Whole Man in a Changing Society."

What goes on, I wonder, in the home of a man who is addicted to attending breakfasts of this sort? What does it do to a wife who has come to accept her husband as the kind of man who wants nothing but quiet at the breakfast table, who will abide no noise louder than the rustle of a turning newspaper page or the clink of a coffee cup, who snaps off any attempt to introduce Hugh Downs into the kitchen and glares at the children's cereal if it emits so much as a snap or pop?

What does it do to such a wife to discover that a man who only mumbles at the news that it looks as though the Fernsprechers down the block are getting their house painted, or that there is a cedar waxwing in the mulberry tree, is suddenly taken with a desire to receive a message from a breakfast table orator?

I will leave this problem to the marriage counselors of whom, goodness knows, there are plenty. Come to think of it the Fraternal Order of Marriage Counselors probably has breakfast meetings too.

I know that doctors do. If you call one, the girl is likely to tell you that he is not in from breakfast yet. This is true of all sorts of occupations. It used to be you could find just about anybody at his office unless it was the day he went to hear a luncheon speech.

Now you reach a man at eleven and he is out of breath.

"Sorry," he says. "I just got here. The after-breakfast speech was fraught with interest but ran a little long."

Benjamin Franklin, as I well remember, was a great advocate, at least in print, of getting up early in order to be healthy, wealthy and wise. It has always been a part of our American creed that there is something praiseworthy about early rising.

But did Franklin foresee that the health, wealth and wisdom was to be gained by listening for half an hour to a lecture on "Africa: Fascinating Continent" or "Whither the Carpet Industry?"

And when our forefathers said it was a good idea to get to work early, what they had in mind was going to the office, not dropping off at the Purple Poodle for rich fellowship and a talk on "New Pathways in Cost Accounting."

I suppose the reason for all this is that there just aren't enough meals during the day to accommodate the number of speeches which the average good citizen feels it is his duty to listen to. Luncheons and dinners are booked for months to come, and breakfast oratory is the only place to turn.

All a man can do is put his trust in the innate good sense of the mainstream of American thought before it is too late.

I would hate to have engraved upon the tombstone of our civilization, this epitaph: "They listened to speeches at breakfast."

(With my customary insistence on being fair, however, I would like to say that one advantage of the public breakfast over the public luncheon or dinner is that the food is almost always better.)

✳ "Yes, dear, I asked the boss for a raise and I think you'll like his answer up until his first 'however.' "

MEETING IS SUCH SWEET SORROW . . .

An expert in efficiency and corporate management says that before anybody calls a meeting or business conference, this question should be asked: "Is this meeting or business conference necessary?"

Well, the reason I am not mentioning his name is that he is a fraud who doesn't know what he's talking about, and simple courtesy forbids exposing him to ridicule. Doesn't he know that if people at the executive level started asking themselves if meetings were necessary there wouldn't be any meetings?

As a result half the highest-priced talent in American industry would be out of jobs. Because we have developed a breed of men (and an occasional woman) who can't do anything else but go to meetings. They are among the most specialized of life forms.

Often you will hear top-level executives, a touch of distinguished gray at the temples, a dignified suggestion of a paunch cleverly disguised by a well-tailored vest, saying to one another: "I'm sorry about young Grinchley. He looked like a prospect for the escalator, sharp mind, good training, pleasant personality, no breath problem, but he just isn't a meeting-goer."

And there will be general agreement that when it comes to meetings, Grinchley doesn't have it.

"As far as his sitting in on a meeting," says a middle-management man, "he might as well be out working."

There is no job ceiling for the man who knows how to conduct himself at a meeting, and he is easy to spot. He knows when to put on his glasses in order to look at the report, when to take them off and chew on the earpieces, when to breathe on them reflectively and polish the lenses with a snowy handkerchief.

He knows, when another man of his own rank or below is speaking, how to shake his head in amused disbelief and put his pencil in his pocket as an indication that nothing worth taking notes on is going to be said.

He even knows what to smoke. If it's to be what the boss calls a real work session, where the plan is going to be hammered out in its final form, he smokes cigarettes, puts a battered pack on the conference table and may even appear in his shirtsleeves.

If it is to be the more common type of meeting in which issues are going to be explored, suggestions tossed around the table like a bean bag, and everyone's thinking is to be shared, he will smoke a pipe. It is the time for profundity, for the man who weighs his words, and in this sort of situation a pipe is a useful tool. Sagacious puffing can prevent a man from saying a lot of things he will be sorry for later.

The cigar is proper for two sorts of meetings. One is the get-together which is primarily social, just sort of getting to know the fellows from the Des Moines branch; the other is when some ruthless action is going to be taken against a colleague or competitor. By chomping a cigar an experienced meeting-man can give the impression of cast-iron ruthlessness without having to do anything ruthless.

There are all sorts of techniques, such as taking up most of the meeting's time with irrelevant discussion and then looking at the wristwatch to indicate that you are a man with better things to do than to sit here jawing all day long.

There is no point in going into all the skills of the good meeting-man. Anyone at all conversant with the subject knows what they are. What matters is that if meetings were abolished the executives who have spent their working lives polishing these skills would be cut adrift. It is not likely that they can be retrained for anything else.

I don't really think that the efficiency expert is going to get very far in eliminating meetings. However, if he would like to make the suggestion almost any company would be glad to call in its top personnel and department heads for a series of exploratory meetings on the subject.

"DON'T FEED THE WASTEBASKET!"

I see that the newest status symbol for executives is the wastebasket with a built-in shredding device which instantly devours anything that is dropped into it. Grinds it right up, converts it into confetti.

The point is that there is an unbelievable amount of spying and snooping going on in the higher levels, both private and governmental. Like if you are president of Enormous Motors and you have been conferring with your chief stylist on the 1960 designs and you jot down "carpeted ashtrays," then wad up the paper and toss it in the wastebasket, you are in trouble.

The custodian is a snoop for Ineffable, Inc. He stuffs the contents of your wastebasket into his lunchbox and smuggles it to G-2 over at your rival's headquarters.

The next thing you know the ads are out and Ineffable's new hottest seller, the Hoptoad III, has carpeted ashtrays and you are in trouble with your stockholders.

Similarly, if you are big in government and you scribble on your Things-To-Do-Today pad: "Escalate in Vietnam," then throw it away, you can be pretty sure that lights will burn late in the Russian Embassy as they iron out the mesasge and shoot it over to Moscow.

So having a wastebasket that chews up whatever you put

into it is a subtle way of impressing visitors with the fact that you are a man who deals in top secrets, industrial or military.

The picture has a certain charm.

A tall man with impeccable grooming and an inscrutable smile stops by your desk and hands you his card: "Fred Fineprint, Regional Agent, All-Heart Health Insurance Co."

You take the card and drop it in your wastebasket. Immediately there is a whirring, chewing, crunching sound as the card is ripped to bits.

"What did you do that for?" the caller asks.

"Can't be too careful," you reply. "A man in my position. Suppose word got around that I was sick and buying health insurance?"

"We don't sell health insurance to sick people," he says rather grumpily, "and besides, those cards cost me three cents apiece."

But you can see he is impressed. He will speak of you to others in awed tones, if only as the nut who macerated his three-cent calling card.

And yet I am afraid that this is one mark of business success which doesn't tempt me. The others—the lovely secretary, the reserved parking space, the stationcry headed "From the Desk of"—I must admit to having, on occasion, coveted.

But not the omniverous wastebasket.

One of the big reasons is that almost everything I throw in the wastebasket I do in a purely tentative manner, sort of on a trial basis. Perhaps somebody has sent me a clipping, and on it, it says, "Why don't you write about this? Ha! Ha!" And I say, "Not on your life. I wouldn't write anything about that with a ten-foot pole," and I throw it into the wastebasket.

Then, along about 3 o'clock in the afternoon, when absolutely no ideas have turned up, I remember what a perfectly splendid clipping that was that somebody sent me, and I up-end myself in the wastebasket in order to dig it out. That's tough enough without finding it all chopped into little bits.

Or the morning will start out with an angry letter from a reader calling me all sorts of unkindnesses and I will treat it with the contempt it deserves—right into old File 13. An hour later I realize that I can't get any work done because it keeps nagging at me: "Did that lady *really* call me what the first hasty reading made me think she did?"

So again I dig it out, and my mind is put at ease. She really did.

Another thing is that I often have to move quickly on my job. As, for instance, when some co-worker looks out the window and gives a lewd whistle, I have to spring up to see what it's all about.

At these times I have a tendency to step in the wastebasket which is bad enough without having a device in there that would chew your leg off.

THE MEDIUM IS THE MONTAGE . . .

The bulletin board, according to the eminent authority Dr. Schnark-Barking, is the world's most ancient form of communication. Contrary to popular belief, it antedates the invention of the thumbtack. We know now that the Phoenicians, and possibly even earlier peoples, used little pellets of mud to stick messages and announcements on walls, and the nomadic desert tribes affixed communiqués to the sides of their tents with camel spittle.

In some offices the bulletin board is starkly austere, confined to messages bearing upon the company's policies: sales figures, orders from the home office as to expense-account procedures, notification of changes in lunch hours and stern admonitions as to who can park where.

Other bulletin boards are almost entirely commercial. Someone in Accounting has lost his keys, car-pool arrangements are desired, a man in Traffic wants to sell a shotgun and another in Plant Maintenance is looking for a good used television. The indication here is that the company does more business inside its own walls than it does with outsiders.

Bulletin boards in offices that employ a large number of women take on a feminine flavor. A lost hankie is pinned in one corner. There are announcements of bridal showers, baby showers, engagements and weddings, plus fluttery thank-you notes resulting from these events. Many of the communications are in green or purple ink.

Then there are the funny businesses, where the bulletin board is a laff riot of gags, cartoons and impertinent comments upon management itself. Here we can assume that the boss is easygoing, possibly fun-loving, and out of the office a lot.

In recent years the bulletin board has become ubiquitous in the home. It bristles with grocery lists, reminders to fix the back door, dental appointment dates and "May be late. Cold roast in icebox. Love." Or even, "Have run off with Cedric. Don't forget blue suit at cleaner's."

Let the other media issue competing claims for their circulations; it's the bulletin board that really carries the vital information to the people.

HEY, KIDS, HERE COMES THE GOOD RUMOR MAN . . .

It is often said when a man retires that he will be missed by his fellow workers, and it must be sadly conceded that there is likely to be a considerable amount of insincerity in the observation.

However, a friend told me the other day that a man in his office had retired and would be missed. He spoke so obviously from the heart that I asked him to explain.

"Was this chap," I inquired, "a hard worker who lightened

the load for others? Was he, perhaps, one who often brought in a lug of tomatoes or sweet corn from his garden to share with his colleagues, or perhaps a clutch of homegrown zinnias for the girls to put on their desks in vases improvised from milk cartons? Perchance he was one of those who made the bleakest day radiant with the warmth of his smile and was always looking on the bright side of life?"

"He was none of these," said my friend. "Sam Sausage was his name and rumors were his game. In all my years of gainful employment he was the greatest rumor man I have ever seen."

"A legend in his own time," I said.

"If not quite," my friend said, "at least it can be said that he started a rumor that he was a legend in his own time. Just as an example, he started a rumor one morning at ten o'clock in our New York branch and got a call about it from Kansas City where it was nine forty-five.

"He used to boast all over New York about that one. He claimed he had spread a rumor so fast that it reached Kansas City before he had even started it. Finally, he ran into a fellow in New York who knew where Kansas City was, and who said that the explanation involved a difference in time zones.

"Unfazed by this, Sam promptly started a rumor that, instead of being an hour behind New York, Kansas City was really an hour ahead. This rumor also spread quickly and is still widely believed along the Eastern seaboard.

"He liked to set himself almost impossible tasks. He would start a rumor in the coffee shop in the lobby and then sprint up the stairs to see if he could beat it to the fifth floor. That was in his younger years, and occasionally he was able to arrive several seconds ahead of the rumor. In later years he had to ride the elevator, which slowed him down, and the rumor invariably arrived before he did.

"Sam particularly delighted in starting a rumor about company policy and having it come back to him from a highly placed executive. If he could get one of his own rumors back from the chairman of the board he was clam-happy for a week."

"I see why he will be missed," I said. "It's too bad he had to retire."

"Well," said my friend, "Sam really wouldn't have had to retire for a while yet, but last month he started a rumor that he was going to retire, and it spread so fast that the next thing he knew they had handed him a gold watch and his last pay check. He phoned me yesterday with a rumor that the watch was turning green. I passed it along in his memory."

BUT ONE STOMACH TO GIVE FOR MY COMPANY . . .

A friend who is in the retirement business says that one of the nicest things about that line of work is that you don't have to participate in any business lunches.

"In the time saved by not having people take me to lunch or vice versa," he reports, "I have read five hundred books, papered the back bedroom and learned the watusi."

He, of course, has put his finger on one of the several things that is wrong with our civilization. If the expression "Let's have lunch" were dropped from the vocabulary of the American businessman, we would have the Great Society by early next week.

The way things are now, if you walk into an office and tell the busy executive that you're the man to see about fixing his desk drawer, he says, "Fine, let's have lunch." The window washer is outside the window washing it, and if he so much as waves, the businessman gets up and calls, "Are you free for lunch?"

When a doctor tells one of these hard-driving executives that he has an inoperable disease, the patient says, "Great, let's have lunch and talk it over."

On the day when the Angel Gabriel gets on the horn to announce the end of the world, many a one is going to say, "That's interesting. How are you fixed for lunch?"

It was thought at one time that stricter interpretation of the internal revenue laws would reduce the number of business lunches, but it hasn't worked out that way. Everybody, it turns out, is deductible for one reason or another.

And this is only fair, I suppose, since in a country where everybody is equal, everybody should be equally deductible. It would never do to have a class of undeductibles, like the untouchables of India, with whom no one would have lunch.

Because the lunch is the outward sign that a man is a participating part of society. Only retirement removes the obligation.

Suppose word got around that Ad Aspera, a rising young executive, was eating lunch by himself.

"He eats lunch by himself" can be as damaging and cruel a thing to say about a man as that he cheats at cards or drinks before breakfast. The minute it gets circulated in the business world, Ad Aspera is no longer regarded as quite sound.

My retired friend says he always played the lunch game. Sometimes he ate three lunches a day just to make sure that he had missed no opportunity to take or be taken.

"The more lunches I ate," he says, "the higher I rose in the company. I started out the same year as Ned Nevermind, a brilliant, quick, hard-working administrator. I went up, up, up in the company, but Ned never got any place because he is a bad lunch man.

"Sometimes when an important connection would ask Ned to have lunch, Ned would answer, 'Why?' This, of course, is unforgivable; you don't ask the reason for a business lunch. You just go.

"On the occasion of my retirement, as I was leaving the office for the last time, I thought back over the thirty-five years and tried to think of anything I had really accomplished. But all I could see was an infinite vista of lunches. I decided right then that my Golden Years were going to be devoted to eating lunch only by myself or with my family."

"And you have found this change enjoyable?" I asked.

"Enormously," he said, pushing his chair back from the table.

"I'll get the lunch check," I said. "After all, I can deduct you as an authoritative source on the pleasures of retirement."

"Thank you," he said. "We must do this again sometime soon." I didn't ask why.

FREEDOM WINS SEAL OF APPROVAL . . .

Recently there appeared in my backyard a tremendous barbecue machine with a hood and a spit and white sidewall tires.

"We are being invaded by suburbia," I screamed to myself. "The last bastion has fallen. I will be out in the yard until snow flies, marinating and broiling and shish-kebobbing and wearing a chef's hat and big asbestos gloves and an apron saying 'Kum-n-Get-It.' I am being crushed by the System. Next comes membership in the Book-of-the-Month Club and watching bowling on television."

But there was a certain fascination about the barbecue machine. I explored it in a spirit of sociological research. Deep in its innards was an Instruction Book. I leafed through it and gained a new insight into America, America.

Not once but several times this booklet said, in effect:

"Barbecuing, above all, must be fun. If it isn't, go inside and cook on your stove."

How are the critics who are always complaining that Big Business is trying to slap us into the straitjacket of conformity going to explain this one? Here was a Big Business, or a Medium Business anyway, saying that if I didn't enjoy their product, so long and lots of luck, no hard feelings.

I am not sure whether golf clubs come with instruction books, but if they do I would like to think they say:

"Golf, above all, must be fun. If it isn't, try tennis or just loafing on the porch."

The manuals that come with automobiles should say, and I hope they do:

"Motoring, above all, should be fun. If it isn't, ride the bus or walk."

What an answer this is to those ill-informed crackpots who think that our society badgers Americans into buying things they don't need and participating in activities they detest merely for the sake of keeping up with the neighbors.

AUNT FRANCIE LOU TRINCH'S PLAN FOR THE PERFECTLY ROTTEN SOCIETY . . .

Aunt Francie Lou Trinch is one of those little old ladies who get up at stockholders' meetings and demand to know when top management is going to quit wasting the investors' dollars. Her favorite complaint is about these Home Economists and Family Advisers and so on that big companies employ.

"Mr. Pomeroy," she says, "I notice that the Octopus Oil Company, in which I own two shares, hires somebody to tell people how to keep the kiddies happy on long automobile trips. What is that in aid of?"

"Well, Mrs. Trinch, and may I say it's nice to see you at our meeting again this year, the corporate feeling is that this sort of effort encourages motor travel, and therefore stimulates the consumption of gasoline, which is what we sell."

"Nonsense, young man," she snaps, perhaps belting him with her reticule. "The way to sell more gasoline is to make family travel as unpleasant as possible. If we do that, then the Mister will go off on a fishing trip by himself while the Miz takes the young ones. That way we double the mileage. We may even triple it if things get so bad that the Miz also takes a trip by herself and the grandparents have to take their sedan out of mothballs and haul the children around the country."

"Your idea," Mr. Pomeroy gasps, "is that the corporation should encourage family discord?"

"Naturally," she says. "This is the business jungle, Pomeroy, and if you can't take the heat, get out of the kitchen. Remember, the family that travels together uses only one gas tank."

Then she arises at the stockholders' meeting of Flukenasser's Flour company and says, "Mr. Attwood, I see top management has employed something named Fanny Flukenasser to advise housewives on how to cook dumplings and pancakes that almost float off the plate?"

"True, Mrs. Trinch," he answers. "The board's thinking on this is that if we help Mrs. Average Housewife learn to cook she will use more of our product."

"Applesauce, young man," she snarls, poking him with her umbrella. "What we need is not a home economist but a home wrecker. We need to persuade the wives of America to cook as badly as possible. When the food gets awful enough, the husband will leave. She will still be there, cooking for the children and using as much flour as ever. Meanwhile he will be eating in restaurants—and restaurants use flour, Mr. Attwood—or some bit of fluff from the office will be having him over to her apartment for meals where he will be stowing away pies and chocolate cakes. There is nothing like an emotional crisis to step up a man's feeding habits."

Top management of the Thicknap Carpet Company, hears as follows:

"What I want to know, Mr. Thicknap, Jr., is why top management wastes the investors' money on hiring decorators to advise people on what color of carpet to buy."

"Why, Mrs. Trinch, I should think it would be obvious that we want our customers to be contented."

"Contented? Poppycock. If we are going to hire somebody to hand out advice, let's have them advise these customers on the worst possible color. Then, after a month, she'll start yelling for new carpeting and he'll say, 'Are you nuts? We just spent a fortune.' And one of them will move out, and whichever one it is will have to get new carpeting for wherever he or she goes to. It is better if he moves because then not only does he get new carpeting but she gets new for the old house because the old carpeting reminds her of him, the beast."

Aunt Francie Lou, I'm afraid, is more worried about her investments than she is about the sanctity of the American home. When I asked her about it, she sniffed, "I'm crazy about the American home. I just think there ought to be more of them, which we can accomplish by splitting up the ones we have. If, as a result, I make more than a crummy seven per cent on some of these dogs I own, so much the better."

To be frank, I don't care a whole lot for Aunt Francie Lou Trinch, but I've got to admit she is an original thinker, economically.

****

WHERE THE DEUCE
IS MY CADUCEUS?

Or: This man isn't well enough to go on sick call.

****

A distinguished psychiatrist has been quoted in the press as saying, "Nothing is a disease until the public decides it is." He was addressing himself to the subject of alcoholism, which has been regarded as everything from a weakness of character to a major crime.

The trend nowadays is to treat it as a disease, which entitles it to a Foundation of its own and, for all I know, a Mothers' March. It is now as O.K. for a wife to call in and tell the office that her husband won't be in today because he has a touch of the booze as it is to say he is down in the back from carrying home all that extra work in his briefcase.

Perhaps we can extend this concept and get the public to decide that golf, as a random example, is a disease. It has to be classified *somewhere*. That way the Blue Cross could cover the cost of the niblick and the greens fee.

My interest in medical affairs has always been somewhat more than that of the next man, unless the next man is a hypochondriac. I came from a family of doctors and was, therefore, raised largely on sample medicines, if any at all. My father was a medical conservative, who handed out pills with reluctance, at least to his family. About the most enthusiastic thing I ever heard him say about any of these tablets or capsules was that he didn't suppose they would do any harm.

I remember one time when I had moved away from St. Louis I returned for a visit without giving my family much notice, and my father apologized because he had to go out that evening.

He said he was making a talk on sex to the students of a private boys' school, and it turned out he did a fair amount of this sort of disseminating of the facts of life.

I mentioned to him that he had never discussed any of these matters with me.

"I never thought you were stupid," he replied. He was a fine man but his judgment was not infallible.

It must have been clear early that I was no more cut out for a career in medicine than in the clergy or civil engineering, the other traditional careers in various branches of the family.

Still, people I have worked with over the years seem to think that medical knowledge is hereditary, and I have often been asked to spell some obscure part of the body, to advise on whether or not hernias should be repaired and to give my guess on a pain in the sternum the size of a quarter.

I rule solemnly on these questions, but, merely as an added precaution, suggest that perhaps a confirming opinion should be sought.

✳ Physicians recommend walking as a means of keeping fit. So why are the doctors' parking spaces always the closest to the hospital?

FOR LIFE'S LOVELY HEADACHES . . .

One of the big companies that makes the little tablets calls attention to the fact that it is about to put out its two billionth aspirin, or maybe it is the 200 billionth. I have mislaid the information, but the exact figure does not, I suppose, make a great deal of difference.

What concerns me is that the image of aspirin is so statistical, so medical. Where is the romance? Where is the heart?

Take the average American family—we all know lots of average American families, don't we—and you can just about tell the story of the years, the triumphs, heartbreaks and so on, in terms of aspirin consumption.

The beer people had an advertising campaign some years back which stressed two themes, "Beer Belongs" and "Beer, the Beverage of Moderation." There were charming vignettes of family life—those memorable occasions, such as Martha Belle's wedding, the burning of the mortgage, the birth of the first grandchild. Each was illustrated by a painting by some master of the Norman Rockwell school showing everybody sitting around the average living room being as average as possible and subtly, nothing blatant about it, belting away at the brew.

There would be, it seems to me, even firmer reasons for a series emphasizing "Aspirin, the Medicine of Moderation," with the sub-slogan "Aspirin Belongs."

I ask those of you who are members of average families to look back over the years and see if I'm not right. The truly memorable occasions have been the ones that called for an aspirin.

That goes for Martha Belle's wedding, and even more for her divorce and her second wedding. It goes for the birth of the first grandchild, and all the subsequent ones.

I won't vouch for the burning of the mortgage because I never knew of an average family that ever paid off a mortgage.

What does a man instinctively reach for when life is really cutting him close to the bone—in moments of joy, of distress, of concern, of passionate involvement of all kinds? Not for champagne or any other telltale beverage. He reaches for good old aspirin.

Why should the cigarette companies get all the romance in their advertising, with the two young lovers running around barefoot over an undeveloped tract of real estate? The payoff is when they discover that they both admire the same brand of cigarette.

How much more poignant if they were to share an aspirin and discover that they preferred the same make, and didn't care if it was buffered or a combination of ingredients.

The Junior Prom, the first day on the job, the evening the boss came to dinner, the promotion, the move to the suburbs, the acceptance into the country club, the audit by the internal revenue service.

These are all rungs on the average family's ladder of success. And they are normally celebrated, not with anything potable, but with aspirin.

It seems to me that the aspirin industry ought to get a little more of that *joie de vivre* into its pitch rather than so much about how many billion tablets they have turned out.

"If it's an occasion," might be their slogan, "it calls for an aspirin!"

If we have a fifteen-minute warning that The Bomb is on the way, after all, the American people will react by taking a shot of acetylsalicylic acid.

✳ Wonderful science foresees the day when there will be artificial replacements for human organs. Some of us, however, have obsolete model bodies that you can't get spare parts for.

DON'T CUT OUT MY APPENDIX, DOC; IT'S THE BEST PART OF THE BOOK . . .

When Lord Moran published his diary describing the physical vicissitudes of Sir Winston Churchill, some people thought it was a violation of the Hippocratic oath, while others regarded it as a valuable contribution to history. I take no sides in the debate, but there is no doubt that it may have an effect on the doctor-patient relationship as profound as that of Medicare.

You and I are nowhere near as historical as Winston Churchill and our doctors do not have titles other than that of M.D. Still, one never knows.

I'm not sure I would want to go to a titled doctor.

Comments such as: "Boy, that's a cold stethoscope you got there, m'Lud," or, "What did Your Grace shoot on the back nine today?" come oddly to the republican tongue.

That, of course, is a side issue. More to the point is that if doctors are going to keep diaries about their patients, we patients had better start retaliating. A great deal of scribbling and talking into tape recorders goes on in physicians' offices. I had always assumed that it had something to do with my medical history. But how can one be sure now that it is not being done in preparation for some posthumous baring of our innermost mechanics, with a movie sale a possibility?

The thing to do, I think, is to take a pencil and pad into the examining room with you. Every time the doctor writes something down, you write something down.

Eventually he will ask, "What are you doing, you idiot?"

"Just keeping a diary, Sam," you reply, "the way you are."

"I'm not keeping a diary," he will snort. "Do you think I'm Lord Moran?"

"No," you say, "and I don't think I'm Winston Churchill, but fair's fair."

He goes on, thumping at your chest, and occasionally making notes. You scribble away at the same time.

"Let me see what you are writing," he demands.

"You first."

"All right," he says, and shows you a piece of paper written in that strange code that doctors write in.

You show him your diary entry for the day:

"Doctor seems unusually flustered and unsure of himself. The least little thing, such as a patient writing notes, seems to upset him. Compulsive need to see what patient is writing indicates—what? Temporary nervousness or severe deterioration? Too early to say."

"Balderdash," he snorts.

You duly jot down: "Disintegration of vocabulary marked by use of words such as 'balderdash' is most distressing. Also should a man of his age snort quite so much?"

The next time you come in, there's a dapper fellow with you in plastic shoes and a silk suit. The nurse says, "Go in the cubicle and take off your clothes."

The man says, "I don't have to take off my clothes, I'm his agent."

The nurse says, "Take off ten per cent of your clothes."

Just then the doctor enters and says, "What's all this?"

The agent says, "It's a great line, baby, write it down."

You say, "I think it's time we ink a pact here, doctor. I want a 25-75 cut on the book and half the movie rights, plus Rock Hudson has to be me in the film if you can't get Richard Burton."

"I'm not writing a book," says the doctor. "Anyway there's

nothing wrong with you. Lose fifteen pounds and quit smoking."

"You're ruining both books," the agent screams to the doctor. "Yours and his."

He turns to leave and the doctor says, "Not so fast there. You look a little liverish. Let's run a series of tests."

The last you see of the agent he is being led off to the laboratory while you and the doctor tear up your notes.

IS THERE A DOCTOR IN THE FAMILY?

I was congratulating a friend the other day because I had read in the press that his daughter was marrying a doctor.

"Hoo boy," I said. "That is really swell. You get a sprain of the bursitis or one of those wheezes in your chest at 3 A.M., your son-in-law is going to come hopping over. He'd better, because if he doesn't your daughter is going to rattle the dishes in the sink the next morning and say, 'You have plenty of time to take care of that lovely divorcee's sprained pinky but can't spare a minute for my own father's heart condition.' A regular doctor in the family. The dream of every man."

He looked glum.

"That's what I thought," he said, "when she telegraphed she was marrying Dr. Whomever. I will have to admit to you that I saw golden acres opening up to my view. I'll confess that after thirty years of marriage the conversation around my house isn't too brilliant. But I figured with my son-in-law the doctor we could talk about this trick knee I got from thinking about going out for football in high school or a funny thing that happened to me one time when I ate an artichoke in Chicago."

"So," I said, "now you are set."

"It hasn't worked out that way," he replied. "The young man arrived at our house and the first thing I do is request an electrocardiogram, just for openers. I didn't want to rush things until we knew each other.

"You know what he turned out to be?"

"No," I said.

"He is a Ph.D.," he replied. "A doctor of philosophy. I started choking when I heard the news and he said for me to loosen my collar. I told him I don't loosen my collar for any-body but a licensed M.D."

"Well," I said, "a Ph.D. lends a touch of class even if he can't do anything about your lumbago."

"We've never had a doctor of philosophy in our family be-fore," he said. "The closest we had was when my niece mar-ried a notary public. Many a fifty cents I saved there for get-ting my signature witnessed. He was a wonderful young fellow. Every time he came by the house I signed my name at least five times. It was a $2.50 evening; I enjoyed seeing him. But what good is a Ph.D. to me?"

"A bad attitude," I told him.

"Perhaps," he said, "but the idea of raising daughters is to have them marry somebody who can take out your appendix or notarize your documents or get you a major appliance wholesale. What am I going to get out of the Ph.D.?"

"Philosophy," I said. "That is what this boy is a doctor of and it will do you a world of good."

"In what way?"

"Well," I said. "Suppose things have been going badly all day; there is not a rift in the clouds. You haven't made a sale and the loan company is pressuring you for the payment. Call up your son-in-law."

"He doesn't have any money," he said.

"No," I said, "but he has philosophy. He can tell you that it is always darkest just before the dawn, that *cogito ergo sum,* and those whom the gods would destroy they first make mad."

"I'm feeling better already," he said.

"Of course you are," I said. "Every family should have a doctor of philosophy. You can get medical advice on any street corner or television program. But philosophy is expensive. And you can never have enough of it. Suppose you had a medical doctor for a son-in-law and you weren't sick. He'd be a waste. But we all need philosophy."

"Do you think he'd make night calls?" he asked.

"For his father-in-law? Of course."

"I'm happy," he said.

"Don't be too sure," I said. "Not until you call your son-in-law the philosopher."

THE WORKER, MORE TO BE PITIED THAN CENSURED . . .

Leading medical authorities are only now getting around to acknowledging that the compulsive worker is as much of an addict as the poor soul who is hooked on alcohol or drugs. Most of us have known of this condition for a long time, and it is a relief to find that overzealousness is now recognized as a disease.

It used to be when we would see a work addict staggering home from the office, his shaking hands, clutching a paper-jammed briefcase, we would say, "Look at Super Sam, the jerk, bucking for vice president."

Now we will be more compassionate, and when we observe a work fiend unable to tear himself away from his desk, even at lunchtime, we will say, "Poor fellow. He is sick."

Conversation turned to this subject in a local center of relaxation the other day. The name of a man who shall be known here only as Norbert X came up.

"Norbert," said one of the company, "is a nice fellow. But he works too much."

"Do you think so?" asked another. "I had always thought he was just an ordinary, social-type worker. You know, the kind that works a little in the morning, but never before breakfast, maybe has a quick shot of work just before lunch, clears off his desk and is out of the office on the stroke of five."

"Well," said the first speaker, "all I know is the way he looks in the morning he must stop off for a few belts of work on the way home. I have nothing against work, understand; in moderation it never hurt anybody. But first thing a man knows he's working forty hours a week, then forty-five and next thing it's out of control."

"Friend," said a gray-haired man who had been listening, "what you say is true. Look at me. Once I was like you fellows. I used to brag that I could take work or leave it alone. I'd put in my hours and quit. But I gradually found that I was sneaking into the office early. When other people arrived they would look at me curiously and I would pretend that I had just arrived. But the truth of the fact was that I had been working.

"A thing like that can't be kept secret for long. I was getting to the office earlier and earlier, staying later. I didn't eat my lunch, or drink my lunch, I worked my lunch. And stayed late, working, while in the little home the martinis prepared by my loving wife grew warm.

"Still I refused to admit that I was a hopeless work addict and made pathetic attempts to cover up the habit. I would not face the fact that work was interfering with my play. I would carry a tennis racket to the office, or hide paper work in my golf clubs. I lied to my wife. When she thought I was at the race track I was sitting in my swivel chair indulging in a disgusting binge of work.

"I can see now that my friends tried to help me. They wouldn't do any work in my presence or even mention the word. I became a solitary worker. When everyone else in the office was relaxing with healthful and invigorating goofing off, I was soddenly plugging away at my work.

"At home my wife would organize bridge games. And I would promise her faithfully that I would not work. But when I was dummy I would go into the kitchen and sneak a quick glance at the September balance sheets or consume an entire stockholders' report. My wife, of course, wasn't fooled, and I cringe when I think of the embarrassment I caused her. I had work stashed all over the house—in closets, under beds —but never in the chandeliers; that was the first place she looked.

"Even the children knew their Daddy worked and often came home in tears from the cruel taunts of their schoolmates.

"Well, that's all behind me now. I haven't worked in thirteen months, twenty-one days and five hours. So you see the craving is still there, but I know I just can't handle the stuff. One job and I'd be off on a spree.

"You young fellows go on back to work if you want to, and I can't say that I wouldn't like to go along with you, if only to watch, but I know better."

And we may be sure that those who had heard this story went very light on the working that afternoon.

ALL THAT READING IS BAD FOR THE LUNGS . . .

I am at least 100 per cent in favor of this ruling that the cigarette people are going to have to put a notification on the pack that "Cigarette smoking is dangerous to health and may cause death." Cigarette labels are awfully dull reading the way they are now.

Not being a man who smokes but, at the same time, being a

man who reads, I often am in a difficult spot. Let's suppose I am on an airplane and have run out of anything to read. I turn to the man in the next seat and say, "Hey there, Mac, you got a cigarette on you?"

He usually says something about its being his last one and I say, "That's O.K. I just want to read the pack."

He says, "Why don't you read one of the many magazines that your attentive hostess will provide?"

And I have to say that I have a thing against reading magazines in leather covers. One reason is that they are always stamped with the name of the airline or the dentist or whoever it is, implying that you are going to steal the thing, which is probably last month's *Popular Mechanics* at best, and the more important reason, which is that if God had meant magazines to come in leather covers he would have made them that way.

After this exchange the fellow rather willingly hands over the pack of cigarettes.

It's hardly worth the trouble, because the only thing to read is the name of the brand and the company that makes it, a brief slogan, a note as to the town of manufacture and some cabalistic tax information.

A man would really be better off rereading the information about what to do when the plane crashes, which is at least exciting.

So I hand the man back his cigarette pack and say, politely, "Thank you very much. Would you care to read the label on my coat?"

Lots of times the man will decline the opportunity, which is a mistake, because the label in my coat is fraught with spine-tingling thrills.

In big letters it says "Warning," then, "This garment is made of synthetic fibers; do not expose to open flame. Do not iron, dry-clean, wash or hang on metal hangers. Keep away from children."

The tobacco interest is being nudged by federal pressure into the mainstream of modern labeling, where all the fun is.

For me it starts in the morning when I read the inscription on the razor blade: "Caution. Rinse, do not wipe."

It gives me something thrilling to think about when I shave. What would happen this particular summer morning, a morning much like any other, if I were to wipe the razor blade instead of rinsing it?

On the breakfast table is the maple-type syrup in a pressurized container. If the people who made it were as unimaginative as the cigarette people they would just put on the label that it is a maple-type syrup and some elevating motto.

Instead, like everything else that comes in pressurized cans, there is a large, red "Danger! Do not squirt in your eye."

I can't think that people who make squirt jars of car polish or pesticide really expect you to aim them anywhere except at your sedan or rose bush. What they do, though, is add zest to their labels by warning you not to aim the nozzle at your eyeball.

So I feel that the tobacco industry is being not only shortsighted but selfish when it resists the Federal Trade Commission's plan to add a little pizazz to the package. At a curbstone guess, 90 per cent of the products we use display warnings of some kind. Two years ago I was given an electric device the purpose of which remains hazy because on the box it says, "Caution. Do not plug in." I have received as much pleasure from the warning as, chances are, I would have from whatever the device may be.

If the reading on cigarette packages is made scary enough, people who don't even smoke may buy them just for the sheer adventure of reading what it says under the skull and crossbones.

A MAN CAN'T EVEN HEAR HIMSELF CRACKING UP . . .

It takes a heap o' squawking, whirring, rattling, tapping, buzzing, ticking, ringing, clacking, creaking, snapping and clicking to make the house moderne a home. Every gadget, be it ever so humble, adds its note to the domestic cacophony.

The poet who had it in mind to live in a house by the side of the road might be content with the location if he wore earplugs to ward off the honking, banging, screeching, whistling, screaming and cries of, "Oh, Mr. Milkman, you forgot the cottage cheese. Yoo hoo! Small curd, please!"

A speaker informed a conclave of the American Medical Association that all this din is causing ulcers and other problems. He thinks that noise control is as much the job of the physician as it is of the acoustical engineer.

It's a sort of nice idea that when we got too jangled we could call the doctor and he would come over with his little black satchel, turn off the garbage disposal, the refrigerator, the television, the dishwasher and the guy next door's electric razor and write us out a prescription: "O.K., everybody, shut up!"

But I frankly see little hope for the anti-noise campaign. Noise has become an integral part of Our Way of Life.

This Christmas, and in all the foreseeable Christmases, Santa Claus needn't worry about whether his clatter is going to arouse the household.

With a jet airplane overhead, the neighbors cracking ice or their knuckles, passing motorists demonstrating the faultiness of their mufflers, and the furnace rumbling mysterious messages, it would take more than a mere thirty-two reindeer hoofs on the housetop to make us even roll over.

A SENTIMENTAL SNIFFLE FOR THE COLD THAT WAS . . .

In the course of one of television's educational commercials, an announcer announced the other night: "The common cold hasn't changed much."

True, in my memory, it hasn't changed any more than the icebox, basketball or the automobile. In other words, its purpose hasn't changed.

The aim of the modern refrigerator is still to keep stuff cold, the goal of the automobile is transportation, and the reason for basketball is whatever it has always been. Misery is the purpose of the common cold, as it always has been and always will be.

A family resemblance remains. A youth who had never seen any automobile before a 1950 model would still recognize a Mercer Runabout as an automobile. After a little investigation, and once he had gotten over the mystery of how come it wasn't plugged in, he might recognize a 1923 icebox as a progenitor of the coppertoned monster in the kitchen.

The same progenitorial relationship can be recognized between the common cold as we knew it in the long ago and the modern cold.

Still, to say that it hasn't changed much seems to me to be stretching a mere family relationship a little far.

There are people who look back nostalgically to the day of the running board and ice delivered in person over the iceman's burlap-insulated shoulder. They will tell you, even, that basketball was a better game when it was played by mere 6-footers.

They are obviously pickles in the pipeline of progress, and I certainly wouldn't suggest that the old-fashioned colds were any better than the colds we have today. I'm just saying they were different.

When I first started getting colds they meant that you could stay home and receive a lot of sympathy. You got to sit around in your bathrobe with your feet in a tub of hot water, and good-smelling stuff was rubbed into your chest and you got an aspirin, a toddy or a hot lemonade from time to time, and you could read Charles Dickens, a great author to read when you had a cold.

Another thing, there were great big handkerchiefs to blow your nose on instead of those little bits of paper they give you these days.

And there was a lot of discussion, held halfway within your earshot, about the interesting way in which you had caught cold. You had gone out without your cap or forgotten your overshoes and somebody would say, "Honestly, I don't know what we're going to do with that boy."

What it gave you was a kind of nice, warm feeling that you had earned your cough and sniffles by bravely disregarding one or more of dull society's stultifying rules.

Young men, stricken in love, used to be able to catch romantic colds by wandering around all night in the rain to ease the pangs of passion. A young man who caught a cold in this fashion was often visited the next day by the object of his adoration, bearing a tureen of broth and her heart.

Today's cold is impersonal and inefficient. No loafing around the house, no Dickens, no toddy. It's one of the cerise-and-mauve capsules on the odd hours and two of the chartreuse-and-indigo tablets on alternate even hours.

You don't lose a day's work or gain an ounce of sympathy. Furthermore, nobody cares where you got the cold. They know you didn't obtain it by going bareheaded or wandering love-stricken in the downpour. The sufferer's adored, far from rushing over with a bowl of soup, figures he probably got the thing from kissing another girl.

It's not even called a cold any more. It's a virus or the Asian flu or, to be really scientific, coryza.

The old-time common cold can no more be retrieved from the mists of history than anything else which society has outgrown. And it's probably just as well. It may have been an inferior product, bacteriologically speaking, but I don't want to be told that it hasn't changed.

NO VISITORS WITH BOOKS ALLOWED . . .

A friend in the hospital says that people have an odd idea about the sort of reading matter to bring him.

"By and large," he reports, "they give me funny books. I have no objection to humor, but it is the toughest thing in the world to pick out for somebody else. The theory, of course, is that something light will cheer me up through the long hours in the antiseptic room.

"Humor never makes the bestseller lists so the buyer has to rely on the judgment of the bookstore clerk and ends up with something like *1001 Jokes for All Occasions*. This is the sort of thing that would dismay the world's healthiest man, let alone a poor sick creature.

"The implication is that you are not only ill but you have suddenly contracted stupidity as well.

"If, by some chance, the book is really funny, then I can't read it, because laughing may be wonderful medicine but it is awfully hard on the stitches."

The anthology or compendium of brief items is generally regarded as the ideal book for the sickroom.

"You can pick this book up, open it anywhere, and start reading," the donor tells the patient, who is tempted to reply, "I already have a Bible."

"There is the dreadful implication," my friend says, "that people who give me a book that can be read a few minutes at a time have very little confidence that I will be around long enough to finish anything bulky.

"What would cheer me up would be if somebody would bring me an unabridged set of the *Decline and Fall of the Roman Empire* in however many volumes and say, 'Now, Sam, what you will like about this is that you can start in right at the beginning and read straight through. No matter how long it takes I know you'll enjoy the socko finish where Nero gets the girl.'

"If that's the way it comes out; I forget.

"It would make me feel that there was somebody who thought I had a few years left to invest in a long-range project."

Another thing this friend objects to is that nobody brings him books with a medical or hospital background.

"They think these would be bad for me," he says. "So I have to buy them myself. I like to get medical books and look in the index to see if my name is mentioned. And they give me a lot of good ideas for new symptoms.

"I also enjoy books about famous medical quacks of history so that I can tell my doctor I'm on to him. Generally, I'm not much for mysteries, but when I'm sick I enjoy books about nurses who poison their patients, or about ungrateful and insidious families who switch the pills from the blue bottle to the pink bottle so that they can inherit the money."

"I didn't know you had any money," I told my friend.

"That's beside the point," my friend said. "Bedside conversation tends to drag and I find I can spice it up if I tell my family that I'm wise to them, they're after my money like a bunch of vultures."

"I brought you a joke book," I told him.

"I knew you would," he said; "put it over there on the windowsill with the others."

"I'm sorry," I said.

"It doesn't matter," he replied cheerfully. "What with

blood tests and meals and therapy and shots and X-rays and idiotic visitors, who has time to read in a hospital?"

"You don't have time to read then?" I asked as a nurse and two interns entered.

"Read?" he said. "They hardly give you time to be sick."

✳✳✳✳

NEW WAVES IN THE MOTOR POOL

Or: Here's my strategy; un-invent the wheel . . .

✳✳✳✳

You and I have noticed that the greatest change in the last few centuries has been in the field of transportation. We have gone from the oxcart to the railroad to the automobile to the airplane, and it's going to get worse. It is a platitude to say that we are making more progress toward reaching the moon than in figuring out some way to get to work and back. The reason is that the Russians aren't trying to race us to work and back.

You know about the built-in biological clocks that the jet airplanes are playing hob with? They are what make you jump up from your cocktail in Addis Ababa and cry, "Hark!" because that's the time they blow the noon whistle on the pickle works back home.

I once knew a girl who was emotionally involved with Paris. She always kept her wristwatch on Paris time. Nice touch. But she didn't pay much attention to it. She'd show up on the dot for lunch even though it was too early (or too late, as the case may be) in Paris. Her heart was on Paris time, but her stomach was on Mountain Standard.

Travelers jet around the world, and wherever they are it's

breakfast time. They're having breakfast every half hour while we are starving to death trying to drive ten miles to the office.

Everybody blames the automobile for the crowded condition of the roads. They forget that without the automobile we wouldn't have any roads.

Anyway, it's all going to be O.K. now because we have a Secretary of Transportation, sitting right up there in the Cabinet with the big boys.

Whoever he is, he's doing a great job. But before the post was created, I discussed the problem as follows:

"The big trouble will be over transportation for the Secretary of Transportation. He'll get a Lincoln or a Pontiac, chauffeur-driven, to ride around in. There will be telephones and a reading lamp in the rear seat, and while he is gliding about he can be studying reports on how tough it is for everybody else to get around in this country.

"I would be great for this job, and I volunteer, even without knowing what it pays. You probably would be fine, too, but we'll eliminate you just to keep things simple. You can always drop by with suggestions.

"They will probably pick a lawyer. They always do. Lawyers know nothing about transportation. Whatever traveling they do is at the client's expense. However, instead of a lawyer, there is the chance that they will pick a real person, which is where we come in.

"Or, rather, where I come in. Because I am a transportee. I am very good at it. I can hold onto a strap with one hand and fold a newspaper with the other while rolling and lighting a cigarette.

"I can imagine the Congressional committee's inquisition of the guy they pick to be Secretary of Transportation. They'll ask him what experience he has had being vice-president of a railroad, traffic manager for a bus line or consulting expediter for an airplane company. If he shows all the blue-chip qualifications at the executive level, he will be approved.

"I know these people. They have their secretary call the secretary of their travel agent to call the secretary of the president of the line to get a ticket.

"They have never been bumped off a flight at Nowhere, Minn., at two o'clock in the morning. They have never been a salesman who arrives on the early train at Ong's Hat, N.J., only to find that his sample case went to Bug Tussle, Tex.

"We are very much aware these days of the need to have the poor on the board of the poverty program and the stupid on the faculty of the university. Let's have some harassed traveling man as Secretary of Transportation.

"It will never happen. They will pick somebody who says that he has commuted to New York and understands the problems. If he's such a big shot he probably commutes in the off-hours.

"The man we need is one of us who has stood in line at train gates, who has alighted from a bus at the wrong station and watched the lights disappear in the distance while trying to figure out how to heft the suitcase two miles to the nearest inhabited spot, who has been stuck on the thruway without a telephone in the car.

"As I have said, you and I agree that a Secretary of Transportation is a good idea. All that possibly you, and certainly I, can hope for is that they put a man in there who realizes that the task of getting from one place to another in this country is becoming increasingly unpleasant.

"But they won't. They'll settle for a man who talks about efficiency, and you and I will be left eating a candy bar in a bus depot, train station or airport in a town we never heard of, wondering where we're going next and asking ourselves why somebody doesn't do something about it.

"Of course, somebody will. There will be the Secretary of Transportation, going over the reports."

Well, this section is about transportation and automobiles and roadside beauty and vacation travel or, as it prefers to be called, tourism which, as an international industry, ranks second only to warfare, to which it bears a close resemblance.

✳ With the highways jammed, railroads cutting services and airlines susceptible to strikes, LSD may be the only way to go.

AN EXCITING AUTOMOTIVE ADVANCE; THE CLUTCH IS ON THE ROOF . . .

It has been widely noted that mankind has a basic, atavistic need to hold onto the top of the automobile with the left hand while driving.

I don't know what anthropology could tell us about the origin of this urge, but it is clear that we all have a deep-seated fear that the roof of the car will blow off or somehow or other become detached as we drive.

It may be that some ancient crustacean ancestor lived inside a shell, like an oyster, and was constantly worried lest his lid be lifted by a predator. So we see today's motorists, almost without exception, driving with the left elbow on the windowsill and the left fist clutching the roof.

I am convinced that one reason for the increase of traffic accidents in the summertime is caused by the spreading incidence of air conditioning in the automobile. With the windows rolled up, a man is deprived of the comforting grip on the roof of his car.

As far as I know, the safety experts have overlooked this

factor or, if they have done any research, have failed to make their findings public.

What happens is that the man who is rolling along in a car with the windows up feels lost, he cannot identify; there boils and churns within him a vague resentment of his environment.

He is like the thumb-sucking child who has been deprived of his woolly blanket. But he is too old to cry.

His subconscious takes over and he drives vengefully, erratically, carelessly. And when the inevitable fender-bending occurs, he springs from his car with loud cries of "Why, you!" and other things.

I will leave it to anyone who has witnessed a collision between an air-conditioned car and an un-air-conditioned car, whether the driver of the former isn't angrier, louder, less well-adjusted. The man whose car is not air-conditioned has been holding the roof down and is at ease with himself and the world.

The air-conditioned man, on the other hand, is all pent up and ready to punch somebody in the nose.

You will ask why this phenomenon doesn't occur in cold weather, when the windows are up, too, and all I can say is that somewhere along the evolutionary trail man discovered he didn't have to hold the roof down in winter. Perhaps the predators that threatened the prehistoric shell of which I spoke didn't prowl when the pond was iced over.

When the safety people finally get around to seeking a solution for this problem, I have one for them. It consists of two inexpensive pieces of equipment. One is a handle which is screwed into the car roof on the inside so that the driver can reach it with ease. Thus, if you get the picture, the window is up, and just within it is this nifty chrome handle that the driver holds onto with his left hand. This quiets his inner misgivings.

But this is not enough. The driver not only needs to feel

that he is holding onto the roof, he needs to feel that other people know he is doing so.

Which leads us to the second appliance. It is, to simplify it, a plastic replica of a human forearm. At the elbow end is a suction cup that fastens onto the outside of the left front window. The "hand" is curved so as to fit over the guttering of the roof. Thus, everyone on the highway respects the motorist as a normal, real American roof-holder. He himself is happy clinging to the inside fixture. The air conditioning is doing its work, and the whole wonderful breakthrough is reflected in fewer traffic accidents.

Who says there are no easy answers to difficult problems?

It's embarrassing to discover that American, which I had always thought of as being the most up-to-date language, is lagging behind others, particularly Afrikaans. Leafing through the new dictionary put out by the *Suid-Afrikaanse Akademie vir Wetenskap en Kuns,* one is attracted by the word *dakvink.*

I immediately put it to use while driving to work.

"*Dakvink!*" I shouted to a burly motorist as I passed him.

After he had caught up with me and crowded me into the curb, he demanded to know why I had called him a ratfink.

"I didn't call you a ratfink, sir," I replied. "What I said was *dakvink,* which in the Afrikaans language means *aloha.*"

He was mollified, although *dakvink* does not mean *aloha,* or even *ciao.*

Dakvink means someone who drives a car with one hand outside on the roof. Isn't this beautiful? Here in America, where the most exhaustive and authoritative psychological research has gone into why people drive with one hand clutching the roof, we have no word for the type.

Out language has, historically, been enriched by appropriating foreign words. So let's swipe this one. A driver who keeps one hand on the car roof is a *dakvink.* We can let it go at that.

THERE'S NO REASON TO LOOK DOWN ON US, JUST BECAUSE
YOU'RE UP THERE . . .

Astronauts Armstrong and Scott assured us that docking the
Gemini in the aft end of the Agena spacecraft was no more
difficult than putting a car in a garage.

I am sure they didn't mean it that way, but this strikes me
as a pretty lofty attitude. Putting a car into a garage may be
an easy matter for a man with training in advanced engineering and experience as a test pilot, but for the ordinary cit it
isn't all that simple.

In the first place, we have to decide what we mean by "car"
and what we mean by "garage." Docking a compact model in
a two-car garage may, I admit, be a fairly uncomplicated maneuver. But parking a 1960 full-size sedan (wasn't that the
year when the Behemoths of the highway bulged to their
maximum width?) in a circa 1923 single-car shed isn't anything to be undertaken with a cry of "Tally-ho" and full
speed ahead on all burners. One yaw and it's leave the car at
the fender mender's tomorrow and take the bus to work.

That's one angle. At least the Gemini and the Agena were
made for each other.

Now the Gemini approached the Agena at the rate of one
foot per second, something on that order. You try to go up
your driveway at that sort of speed and the neighbors are passing it around that you had another one of those long, drinking lunches today. For the sake of the reputation, the motorist
has to bust right up to the garage like he has all the confidence in the world.

The result of this is the sort of crunch that only a bicycle
can make. It may be that astronauts run such a tight ship
around home that the children's vehicles don't lurk in the

middle of the garage, but the average Daddy has to be very cautious in this matter.

In addition, running over a bicycle or a trike, or any sort of tot transport, is always the fault of the Daddy at the wheel. I don't know why this is so, but it is a traditional rule of the road.

"Waah, he roont my bike," when uttered in a piercing voice, is an indictment that easily sweeps aside such feeble rejoinders as "What was that blankety-blank bicycle doing in the middle of the driveway?"

I know a man who once ran over a new clothes hamper in his garage. It roont the clothes hamper and his wife said, "Waah!"

When he inquired mildly as to why a blankety-blank clothes hamper should be in the garage, his wife explained that she had been out slaving at the canasta table and had left a note to the delivery men to put the clothes hamper in the garage.

It was, she pointed out, the only place to put it.

In the case of the astronauts, the unfortunate disturbances that occurred after the spacecraft had docked were attributed to a mechanical malfunction with no human error involved.

With a man docking his car in his garage, pilot error is always the first, and usually the only, assumption.

Armstrong and Scott skillfully undocked when they discovered they were in trouble, and this often happens when it comes to putting a car in the garage.

The second the docking maneuver has been accomplished and the driver unbuckles his seat belt with visions of relaxation ahead, there comes from the kitchen window various "Yoo-hoo, Sams."

Wearily he rebuckles the belt and disengages the car from the garage. A "Yoo-hoo, Sam" means a trip to pick up the laundry, a child, or a bottle of milk. Many veteran car dockers, in fact, back the car out as soon as they get it in, because they know from experience that the first time isn't going to take.

They could have told the astronauts as much.

Docking two spacecraft in the limitless void isn't easy, and I have to salute the boys for their modesty in saying that it was just like putting a car in the garage.

But couldn't they have been modest without downgrading a maneuver that many an ordinary mortal spends a lifetime doing wrong?

WHO'S AT FAULT, DETROIT OR PROVIDENCE?

A great deal of attention is being paid to the question of what the automobile industry ought to do to make the product safer. Maybe we're approaching this thing from the wrong end. After all, there are only a certain number of things you can do with a motorcar, the basic design of which is established by some sort of immutable natural law.

But what about people? It seems pretty obvious that we are badly designed for the motor age. Like the head up on top of the neck, which is just asking for a whiplash injury.

If the neck were eliminated, as it has been in the case of some wrestlers, it would be a major step toward traffic safety. As it is, the head bobbles around, and if it isn't being snapped backwards it's going forward and cracking the dashboard. Maybe we ought to go beyond eliminating the neck and sink the head down inside the chest where it would be protected.

Now there are those who will say "Hold on there," and "Just a minute." They will say that the design of the human body is just as much a part of the divine plan as that of the automobile.

And yet we seem to be incessantly reading about how some

scientist is unlocking the key to life, unfolding the mystery of the genes and, in general, getting ready to do humanity over.

To assume that the human body cannot be rejiggered in the noble cause of accident prevention is to be out of sync with the current thinking that man can do just about anything he programs his computers to do.

Now, of course, these changes can't be made overnight, but it doesn't look as though any major alteration in the safety design of automobiles is going to come like a bolt of lightning either.

If it is to be a long-range program, then it is not too soon to start making long-range plans. Take the matter of arms. Is two the right number? You may say yes, because that is the number we have traditionally had. But if a driver is going to steer, light a cigarette, dial the radio, hold a road map, rap the noisy child on the head, all while waving one hand outside the car, as so many motorists seem to find it necessary to do, four or five arms would seem more efficient.

Here is a good juncture at which to point out that difficult decisions will have to be made. The Conference on Redesigning the People of the United States (CORPUS) will have to approach these questions with a great deal of thoughtfulness.

More arms may be handy for the driver, but the pedestrian is another matter. Extremities are a handicap. When he is hit by a car they tend to be broken or contused.

The ideal pedestrian, I suggest, should be almost completely spherical. He should have the minimum extension of arms and legs to enable him to trundle about and perform necessary daily tasks, but these should retract on impact so that he would roll when struck.

Since most of us are pedestrians at times, motorists at other times, it obviously would be a bad idea to design two different types of people. All these matters would have to be threshed out.

But anything worth doing requires a little effort. And there would be side benefits. A completely redesigned human body would be a powerful boost to the economy. Clothes, furniture and a lot of other things would be obsolete.

We are told that in modern society the humanities lag behind science, but here is a field where science needs to catch up. The world's artists have been redesigning the human figure for several years now, while science drags its feet.

No matter what Detroit decides to do, we'll never really be safe in these outmoded bodies.

DEDICATE A CHUCKHOLE TO POSTERITY . . .

The Interstate highway system is nearly completed, and, of course, those of us who like to dash around to visit Grandma or check up on a football game or sell a gross of the product in one town or another are pleased.

On the four-lane superhighways we can get from place to place in half the time it used to take. It is safer, too. In order to have an accident on the new highways you have to be really trying. It's still possible, but it isn't easy.

This is what we are building for our posterity, and we want nothing but the best for them.

However, I wonder if we aren't depriving them of some of the character-building experiences which produced the great leaders of the nation such as you and me. Will motorists of the future, as they speed in limited-access comfort and safety across the land, appreciate what it was like in our day? If they don't, how can they understand what sort of people forged the legacy which was handed down to them?

It was often said to my generation that our principal handicap was that we had never personally known what it was to come overland in the Conestoga wagons. We never had to ford the rivers or form the prairie schooners in a circle at night with the women and children in the middle.

This lack in our upbringing caused us to drift from the verities of the founding fathers. Compared with the pioneers who fought their way West despite famine, drought, blizzards and hostile Indians, we are a soft generation. It is too late to firm us up, but we can at least avoid making the same mistake. In our zeal to see that our children and grandchildren travel swiftly and safely across the land are we purloining their birthright? Are we conspiring to make them even softer than we are ourselves?

My proposal is that a few stretches of primeval highway be set aside as National Monuments so that motorists in the decades ahead will know how it used to be. We realize now that we did not preserve enough widerness areas or virginal grasslands. And we are sorry for it.

Our great-grandchildren, riding secure the antiseptic highways of the future, cannot know what it was like to spend an hour behind three tailgating trucks with the bright lights of approaching traffic in the eyes and the blinking of neon signs confusing the peripheral vision.

On the Federal arteries of the future, bypassing cities and villages, they will never have experience with the speed trap and the justice of the peace who knows only one legal ruling —if you have an out-of-state license you are guilty.

The thrill of the S-curve with the rain-slick blacktop and the narrow bridge at the end will only be something they have read about in history books, the way we read about the Indian ambush at the pass.

Getting lost on a half-marked detour 19 miles from anywhere will be as unimaginable to them as finding one's way across unexplored mountain passes is to us.

Let us, then, establish, before it is too late, a few sections of U.S. 40, or some similar highway, in their pristine condition.

As the years go by, they will be not only educational, they will be tourist attractions.

People who now travel long distances to see reconstructed pioneer forts or quaint villages will pay fees of $1.50 a head to travel on the sort of highways their granddaddies (meaning us) used to drive. These are the roads that built great-souled men (such as you and me). Progress demands that they shall go the way of the Santa Fe Trail, but some examples must be preserved if we expect posterity to have any respect at all for the rigors of these olden days.

NIT-PICKING FOR PICNICKERS . . .

There is a myth that a better picnic spot is always around the next curve. Although the belief has been widespread for years, it was not until 1966 that any serious research into the matter was done by a task force working under a Federal grant.

The field work was simple. Researchers would approach picnicking families and ask, "Folks, why are you eating your egg-salad sandwiches here?"

Invariably the reply was, "Because there is a better place around the next curve."

Then the scientists would drive around the next curve and look. In only 6.8 per cent of the cases investigated was there in actuality a better place. In 90.3 per cent the place was worse. The remaining 2.9 per cent represents those cases in which task-force members couldn't agree whether the place was better or worse, and also indicates the presence on the team of Associate Professor Kelp, who held that there was no such thing as a good place for a picnic.

The researchers also went back in the direction the picnickers had come from, retracing their route, and found out that, in almost the same proportion, they had passed up better sites than the one where they finally landed.

One family, indeed, was traced all the way back to its own front yard, which was found to be the best picnic spot the researchers had seen all day. They ate their lunch there, except for Associate Professor Kelp, who drove downtown to the Harvard Club.

NOTHING'S RIGHT ON THE WAY TO ANYWHERE . . .

Every transit strike revives the matter of car pools. Suburbanites, are very properly reminded that if they are going to drive into the city they should take some neighbors with them. The car carrying only the solitary driver through traffic is an inefficient mode of transportation, as we all realize, although we will fight to the death for our right to drive as we please, convinced, as we are, that this freedom must surely be guaranteed to us in the Constitution.

Most of us have, I suppose, had some experience with car pools. They are tricky things.

In the first place, there is always somebody in the car who has to drop something off at the cleaner's. There is the brief honk (or *honque* in more elite neighborhoods), and this fellow comes scuttling out laden with three suits, the living-room draperies and his wife's coat.

"I hope you don't mind, Sam, and the rest of you gang of buddies," he says, "but would you mind stopping off at the Bong Tong Cleansers? Just take a minute, right on the way."

"Not at all," says the driver, name of Sam. The fellow scrooches in with his load and the ride continues for a few blocks, when Sam asks casually, "Where is this Bong Tong

Cleansers, Norm? I'm not too sure I remember it exactly."

"Right on our way," says Norm, "except that you better take a right at the next street as it's more or less over toward Nowhere Gardens."

"Say," says a previously silent passenger named Edmund, "as long as we're going that far over, would you mind swinging a little bit back in the direction we came from as I promised my insurance man I'd drop by and pick up a calendar he's been holding for me."

Other errands occur to everybody else, except the driver, and it is somewhere along toward noon before anybody gets to work.

There is also the problem of plain ordinary incompatibility. Most men can get through the breakfast hour all right, keeping the grouchiness in check and even giving the wife and children a fairly cheerful goodbye peck on the cheeks.

In his automobile, by himself, he can work off his hostility on the radio pushbuttons, talking back to the newscasters and changing stations whenever a commercial or a contest comes on. By the time he is at work all the hatred has been drained from his system.

But with others in the car, there is bound to be one genuinely cheerful person who will say, "Don't change that station. I want to see how much money is in the Mystery Jackpot," or who will whistle along with the music.

And the driver will find himself saying polite things, such as "Why, not at all, Fred," or "You're paying your share of the gas, Alfred, you call the tune."

By the time he gets to work he has so much surliness built up inside him that he snaps at his secretary and may irritate his ulcer with a martini for lunch.

Then, of course, there are the navigators. You have a man at the wheel and four navigators, each with a different idea. One thinks that by going around behind the church and crossing the tracks this side of the old depot you can miss the shift change at the ratchet factory and pick up a straight shot down Elm Avenue without a stoplight.

Another says this is nonsense. The wise move is to circle back through Nottingham Estates and pick up the expressway as far as the Bottomley exit.

Others . . . But no matter, you get the idea.

There are, too, the wrangles about whose turn it is to drive tomorrow. Actually it is Fred's, but his wife needs the car to go to the beauty parlor, and there is persiflage that turns into bitterness.

Many car pools, I know, have survived the years. The same is true of many marriages. But in neither case is it easy.

ARE WE TO ALLOW PHOTOSYNTHESIS TO RUN WILD?

Congressman Sludgepump rises and is recognized.

Mr. Speaker:

I am sending to the clerk a copy of a bill which I have marked HR: 16897. It has for its purpose the regulation of the costly, wasteful and generally unsatisfactory coloration of the leaves in the autumn, or fall as it is known in some parts of the nation.

For many years I have been concerned about this undisciplined affair which, for a few weeks, makes a garish display upon the hillsides of our country with little regard to the needs, or indeed the wishes, of the farmer, housewife and small businessman.

I would like to read a letter from an eleven-year-old constituent, Miss Susy Belle Sausage, who writes me as follows:

"Last week my father was driving us in the country. My mother was along and my Aunt Delphine and my brother, Ned, but you can forget about him.

"Just as we were going around a curve on highway No. 50 my mother and my Aunt Delphine screeched look at the beautiful maple or maybe it was a oak. Anyway, my father thought there was a bee loose in the car or somebody had dropped a cigarette on the upholstery when he heard the yelling and he screeched on the brakes and the car swerveled around and might have hit this big truck coming the other way if it hadn't been for my father's razor-sharp reflexes as he is fond of describing them.

"He says that all this color in the trees is a menace to traffic safety especially if there are screechable females in the car.

"I asked him if it was such a danger why didn't somebody do something about it, and he said that is a good idea and somebody ought to write to our Congressman and I said who is that and he said he didn't know, but I looked him up and he is you.

"So won't you please make a law that there shall be no more red, yellow or worse trees, especially on curves? It will save the lives of many little girls and their families and even their brothers, if you think that is important.

"Sincerely, Susy Belle Sausage, age 11."

I wish to say to honorable members on both sides of the aisle that this is a human document which should not be lightly disregarded. Safety on our highways has always been one of my primary concerns, as it has been of many other distinguished and able members.

There are other considerations as well. The autumnal foliage stimulates many otherwise nontroublesome citizens to the practice of poetry. In these days of crisis at home and abroad, it is an economic and social waste to have poetry widespread in the land.

The Russians and the Red Chinese, I am convinced, do not indulge themselves in this manner. Does a poem on the beau-

ties of the sumac and the sassafras marching across the land-
scape like an army with crimson banners help us get to the
moon? I think not.

Have you ever asked yourself this question: "If I were a
Communist, what would I do to bring the great and powerful
United States to its collective knees?"

If you have asked yourself this question, I am sure you have
answered yourself: "Why, I would do everything in my power
to lull the citizens of the United States into an apathetic and
complacent attitude of euphoria and good spirits."

And this is precisely what the flaming leaves accomplish
every October. You will often see, as I have, grown men, solid,
respectable leaders of vast enterprises, dynamic participants
in this free economy of ours, gazing at an oak or a sugar
maple with looks of silly rapture on their faces.

If you ask them why, they will say that just looking at the
beauty all around them makes them "feel good." We cannot
afford for people to "feel good" in these desperate times, unless it is some accomplishment in Outer Space or Southeast
Asia that inspires them. If the trees weren't showing off in this
manner, there would be a lot more solid accomplishments
this time of year.

But the heart of the matter is that this annual riot of color,
this blaze of pigmentation in the countryside, is absolutely
unregulated. Each state, each county, indeed each tree, goes
its own way, without the aid of constructive planning from
Washington.

Can we tolerate this sort of arboreal anarchism? To ask the
question is to answer it.

No truly Great Society can depend on the whims of any
species of vegetable, no matter how large.

My bill is not a radical one. It merely calls for the appointment of a committee to study ways and means for requiring
that trees abandon their uncontrolled exhibitionism and, in-

stead, make the contribution to our society of which, under proper Federal supervision, I am sure they are capable. Thank you. (*Applause*)

MAYBE BIRDS WISH THEY COULD WALK AS WELL AS PEOPLE CAN . . .

I hope that these people in Delaware who are working on a way for man to fly just by flapping his arms (which is somewhat an oversimplification of their plan) think through what it implies before they go much further.

Now we know it's the truth that the desire to fly, to tumble about in the freedom of the air and to feel the exhilaration of flight lies very close to the human heart. We can all remember when we were little freckle-faced, stub-toed boys and we would lie on the side of the hill and watch the ivory-billed woodpecker or some other species of bird which is now as extinct as that species of little boy.

We would say to ourselves, "Boy, it would be keen to fly like that and maybe go over to the county seat and perch on the statue of General Junius Kumquat, like a pigeon."

It may not be news to some of you that men do fly. But it's not the same thing, lashed into a metal tube with piped-in music and delicious meals in your lap. We can fly, all right, but it means making a reservation and getting to the airport a half hour ahead of the theoretical flight time. And it costs money, too.

All of this is for the birds, but not *of* the birds. If birds had to go through what people do in order to fly, you'd see more of them riding trains or buses, believe me.

Not wishing to knock the Wright brothers, but flying inside a machine and worrying about the credit cards and the weight limit on the luggage and how to get from the airport to civilization isn't what Leonardo da Vinci and the rest of us have had in mind.

Nor, at least as far as I'm concerned, is this thing of being pushed out of a plane for a long drop with a parachute. Devotees of this sport are enthusiastic about it. However, I agree with John Seney, who is pursuing the project in Delaware, that it's not flying unless you can take off under your own power.

What we want is to be like Eric Knight's Flying Yorkshireman. We yearn, deep down, for the leisurely flight around the room, the careless ascension over the traffic-jammed highway. This, to most of us, is flying.

After all this has been said, we must face the fact that just because we all want to do bird imitations doesn't mean that it would be good for us, or for society.

Think for a minute what it would do to the elevator industry if everybody could fly up to the floor of his choice on his own. Maybe you don't own any elevator-company stock, but lots of widows and orphans do, and what good is it going to do them to be able to fly if they are going broke at the same time?

Suppose your office is on the fifteenth floor and you have Miss Skirmish there in the outer room to delay unwelcome visitors such as bill collectors or process servers. You may think it would be nice if you could just step out on the ledge and wing away like some auk or other. On the other hand, it won't do any good for Miss Skirmish to tell these people you aren't in, when all they have to do is fly up and peck at your window and they can see you sitting there.

I assume we will still need airliners for long and swift trips. Hazards already abound, as when a plane hits a Canada goose. It is going to be even worse when Flight 802, coming in for a landing, collides with a forty-seven-year-old insurance salesman fluttering home for dinner.

And the mind boggles at what might happen if people in large numbers started sitting on telephone wires.

⁂ The supersonic airliners will have windows, although the only thing you can see outside a plane flying at 70,000 feet is something you're almost certain to wish you hadn't.

DO YOU HAVE A COPILOT IN YOUR ROOM?

Do you remember the olden days when we country boys would come to town and there would be this gas lamp in the hotel room and, having never seen the like, we would blow it out and there would be all the resultant asphyxiation? Or we had never seen electricity and would cut the cord leading to the light bulb?

Of course you remember all that, and you think we are too sophisticated any more to be unable to cope with the wonders of a hotel room. But don't bet on it.

Today the hotel room is so complex you can't run it without an instruction manual and a thirty-minute lecture by the bellman.

The guy that carries the grip used to come in, turn on the light, open a couple of doors, showing the closet and the bathroom, put the key on the dresser, pocket his tip and exit merrily.

But no longer. Instead he calls sternly for attention and goes over the room, explaining every pushbutton and dial, from the thermostat to the machine that makes the ice cubes. He has to tell you which ones it is O.K. for the layman to touch and which ones to let alone. It would be an exaggeration to say that it is a briefing as complete as that given the astronauts, but it comes pretty close.

And the guest had better pay attention.

I was spending the night in a hotel a while back, and I felt that I could sleep better if the television weren't blatting. I have seen a television set before and I felt that I was competent to turn one off. I pushed, pulled or twisted everything that protruded from the box. It went serenely on. I was reduced to the final humiliation. I called the desk to admit that I hadn't paid close attention to the instructions, or had anyway failed to take notes.

Where you had to turn the television off was a switch set into the head of the bed. Very convenient, of course, but also confusing to a man who had come to terms with television sets on the basis that they had an On-Off switch somewhere on their chassis, not clear across the room.

Also, telephoning the desk isn't the simple thing it once was. You have to have a pretty accurate idea of what you want. There is one number for the valet and another for room service and another for reservations, and so on. It's no longer a matter of picking up the phone and telling the nice lady you want a chicken sandwich, your suit pressed and an outside line.

You have to study the fine print before you dare lay a finger on the dial.

As I have said, if you miss one syllable of the bellman's lecture you can end up with a temperature of 97 degrees in the room, or you'll find out at two o'clock in the morning that the ice machine has filled the bathtub with cubes and shows no signs of quitting.

The flight instructor who shows you to your room—and often he doesn't even carry the luggage, that's handled by another subsidiary—will inquire, "Have you stayed with us before, sir?"

If, like me, you are the type who tries to bluff through situations of this kind by pretending to a sophistication you don't possess, you will say, "Oh, yes, I have stayed with you incessantly. Do you take me for some sort of huckleberry or other?"

Often the uniformed chap is kind enough not to just walk

away and leave you in your ignorance, as he might well do. Instead he will ask, "All right then, wise guy, sir, where's the bed?"

You look around confidently, assuming that even you can find a bed in a hotel room. There's no bed.

"That's funny," you say. "I must have stayed in a different kind of room last time."

"They're all alike," he says.

"Do I get three guesses?" you ask.

By this time he is weary of the game and shows you what article of furniture the bed pops out of it you know the combination. There is a round of winks, chuckles and tips, and about midnight when you get ready to go to bed you have to call somebody or other and ask where they hide the pillows.

The modern hotel room is a wonder of comfort and convenience. Living in one is no more difficult than flying a four-engine jet. But, in both cases, you'd better get all the expert advice possible before you try to operate one on your own.

FORGET ABOUT COLUMBUS, THE EARTH IS SQUARE . . .

We might as well face it. In the lengthening decades ahead we will be competing with other planets for industries and population and universities and all the other amenities which at the moment are merely up for grabs between cities and states.

And we have a terrible handicap. The name of the place.

Earth.

How does that grab you? Does that sound like the kind of place you'd want to move your factory? Oh, it's all right. It has a kind of solid squareness about it, like, say, Kansas City.

But it's terribly short on glamour.

It's the Peoria, the Keokuk, of the solar system. Both good towns but they've been worn slick as vaudeville jokes.

Suppose you're working for a company in the home office on Venus and the word comes through that you're being put in charge of the Earth branch. It's a nice promotion, salary-wise, but is it worth it as far as your family is concerned?

"Earth?" your wife shrills. "It's the jumping-off place. Nobody lives on Earth."

You mention that there are several billion, but you know what your wife means. Nobody who is anybody.

You point out to her that she has never been to Earth so how can she be sure it's that bad?

"Just from the name," she sobs. " 'Earth.' Say it over to yourself a few times. It's nothing; it's nowhere. Talk about Venus or Mars or Jupiter or Saturn or even little old Pluto, which is kind of cute, and you have places that sound like you would want to live there.

"Remember last year when Madge's daughter married that Earth boy, and all the jokes? Jokes, but Madge like to cried her heart out. Her baby going to live on a place called Earth. Even at the wedding reception, people coming up and saying, 'I've been to Earth. I spent a week there one Sunday,' things like that."

I personally happen to be a big booster of the Earth. For variety of climate, for culture, for general friendliness of the people and convenience—it's not too big or too small—I think it's about as dandy a planet as there is. But the name is a drag.

My guess is that, as the solar system becomes all one big community, people will be hesitant to admit that they come from Earth.

They'll say that they come from the Greater Moon area or just south of Neptune.

A lot of us who love the Earth are going to get awfully tired of having to explain that it's not as bad as it sounds and having everybody laugh when they hear the name. So maybe what we had better do is settle on a better name.

Sentiment is all very well, and there's no use arguing that many of us who are second, third or fourth generation Earthmen have a sort of attachment to the name. But, if we're going to compete in the big time, we might as well admit that it has a bush-league sound about it.

We have no trouble at all thinking up attractive names for our subdivisions—Avalon or Somerset or Brookledge. Classy, you know?

Let's get something of the same nifty nature for Earth before it's too late.

FOR EVERY CITY, A DEPARTMENT OF KIDNAPING . . .

How to build up a Really Great city is the constant study of people who want to live in that kind of place. They put a lot of thought into how to get more people to move to their city so they can say they now have more people than Cleveland or Amarillo or whatever city it is they think they are in competition with.

There are many ideas about how to attract people, as with an opera festival or sparkling-clear drinking water or a zoo or a big-time football team.

My thinking is that the best way to get people in a town is to trap them. And I am not alone in this, because many cities seem to be making pretty good-sized strides in this direction.

It occurs to me that the reason New York is so enormous is that people go there from Wherever, Neb., and disappear into a subway station and are unable ever after to find their way back to street level, let alone Nebraska.

Or a family from Let Alone, Iowa, will be touring around the metropolis and somehow or other get into Brooklyn and start asking questions, and it will just eventually seem simpler to settle wherever they wind up. They write the folks back home to send the household goods, and Iowa's loss is New York's gain.

Who knows how many people are roaming the interminable freeways of Southern California, hopelessly seeking an egress, occasionally pausing for an avocadoburger?

Where does the census bureau count these folks? It would seem unrealistic to continue to regard them as members of the community of Otherwise, N.D., from whence they set out. They must, it seems to me, be registered as swelling the burgeoning population of megalopolitan Los Angeles.

Lesser communities must pattern themselves after the great cities if they are to remain competitive. They, too, must develop traps, and I am heartened to observe that they are moving in this direction.

Airports, for example, are excellent people traps. People who have somehow or other missed flights or been bumped out of their reservations at the airports of this nation often find it easier to settle down than to fight the battle of trying to get somewhere else.

You will notice, as the great silver bird lets down at any airport, clusters of little homes. They weren't there when the airports were built. They are the homes of people who got trapped in the terminal. The skycaps sell real estate on the side.

Modern four-lane highways enable you to whisk yourself across the nation and through the average city, unless you hit one that has some genuine enterprise.

The go-ahead communities offer you a choice, about a mile outside of their city limits, of three branches marked "Barfleigh Heights Thru Tpk," "East Clampley Overturn," and "Trenchant Avenue Truck Route." No matter which one you take you end up amid warehouses, breweries and more signs saying "One Way" in contradictory directions.

The wise motorist gives up. He knows he is trapped, and the family sends home for the mother-in-law and the kids' bicycles.

Any ambitious city today can hope to keep abreast only by establishing a wide-awake dynamic Bureau of Tourist Entrapment.

✳ In a nice switch, the returned travelers down the street were entertained by the neighbors who showed them color slides of burglars ransacking their house while they were away.

SOME DAYS YOU CAN'T SEE THE ISSUES FOR THE BIRDS . . .

The time rolls around when a man gets a little panicky and realizes that if he doesn't hurry on and write the vacation column it isn't going to get written. The problem is what kind to write.

Probably the easiest is the family vacation column where you make fun of your wife and kids and tell about hilarious breakdowns of the automobile and that sort of thing. The only trouble is that unless a man is an irresponsible sensation-monger he must write only the truth, and the truth is that I didn't take any trip with my family this summer, and if I had, the children, to say nothing of my wife, are mostly too old to do anything very funny.

Currently, the most popular vacation column is the one written by the deep-dish brains of Washington. It begins with a folksy and bucolic dateline, something like Pumpkin Hill, Md., or Forbes's Forge, Va., or Ned's Notch, N.H., and it goes like this:

"Here amid the August haze of the Rappanoodnick Mountains, with the sandpipers chirping in the furze and the wings of a Tufted Thrip making lazy circles in the sky, one gains a new perspective.

"In the rat race of the power struggle in Washington one tends to lose that perspective which one can only recapture under the conditions outlined above. Here, far from the frustrated ranting of hawks and doves one may concentrate instead upon the songs of [Note to Editor: Insert names of two birds. There's no dictionary up here].

"A man finds here a peace, a contentment, etc., etc. . . ."

Again honesty raises an obstacle. Most Washington oracles seem to own one of these rustic retreats where they can go and get away from the hustle and bustle and the constant banging away at the same old confusing issues—and give their readers a nice rest, too.

But I have no such spot in which to receive the benison of sylvan psychiatry.

This may be the year that the vacation column doesn't get written.

MAKE MONEY! BE AN ANTI-TRAVEL WRITER . . .

While other forms of literary endeavor languish, the travel article is flourishing. Perhaps because the practitioners of this art have taken their style, apparently, from the anti-novel, featuring the anti-hero. So what they produce is the anti-travel piece, as seen by the anti-tourist tourist.

The actual job of writing is ridiculously easy, particularly if you write about the United States. One simply starts out with the premise that, no matter what one sees, one isn't going to like it. (Referring to yourself as "one" hits almost exactly the correct supercilious tone.)

An integral part of the premise is that, while presumably writing for tourists, one despises tourists.

Tourists, in the world of travel writing, come in pairs, and each pair has one dominant and one dominated member.

As an example:

"On the rim of the Grand Canyon one's sensibilities were offended by a fat female member of the species *Tourista Americanus* who had crammed herself into tight toreador pants and wore open-toed gold sandals, totally unsuited to the terrain or to the general esthetic ambiance.

"O.K., Charlie," she rasped in the nasal tones of the Middle West to her mate, a mousy man in a flowered sports shirt. "So look at it. For this you make me pass up Vegas to see a hole in the ground."

"One could not repress a shudder."

Or:

"One finds it difficult to report with any perceptiveness upon the treasures of the National Gallery when one has had one's ears lacerated by the Midwestern rasp of a large cigar-smoking tourist in a wide, flowered necktie; 'O.K., Velma, now we seen the pitchers, let's go get a drink.' His wife, a mousy woman in flowered chintz, dumbly acquiesced."

For the beginning travel writer it is wisest to identify all tourists as from the Middle West. It gives the reader a sense of security. There is no point in confusing him with loud-mouthed tourists from Connecticut, Oregon or, for that matter, England. He won't be entirely sure that he knows what you are talking about. (Incidentally the children of all tourists are most easily referred to as "brats," preceded by a mixture of pejorative adjectives.)

Nor is it good form to say anything nice about the natives (except once in a while, to make the tourists sound worse). If they do not try to sell one souvenirs or food, they can be written off as backward; if they do, they are obviously greedy or money-mad.

In the matter of historic shrines: If they are well kept and restored to their original condition, one may call them "commercial" and remark patronizingly about the American mania for reconstruction. If they are shabby, one laments the shortsightedness of a nation that lets its heritage disintegrate in this shameful manner.

Of any historic or scenic spot, it is a safe plan to work in something about the roads leading to it. If they are rough, curving, or in any way not up to interstate standards, one decries the stupidity of those responsible for making the attraction so inaccessible. On the other hand, if the roads are good, one writes bitterly of broad ribbons of concrete completely ruining the charm of the countryside.

If the food is plain, one regrets the inability to get a really great soufflé or bouillabaisse. If it pretends to be continental cuisine, one is appalled by America's snobbish mania for nonindigenous food and longs, in print, for a good honest hamburger.

If the prices are high, it is extortion; if they are cheap, then the place is appealing to the sort of tourist who is really not one's sort.

These are just a few guidelines to writing in the manner of the most successful travel writers who display as their motto: "If You Can't Knock It, Don't Try It."

HISTORY AS NEAR AS YOUR MAILBOX . . .

We are all interested in spreading a love for history, especially among the younger element, and museums and restored homesteads of the great are proliferating. The danger, it seems to me, is that we may run out of historical mansions and battlefields and old borax mines.

Furthermore, the history isn't very evenly divided in this country. Some areas, such as New England or Virginia, have history virtually wall-to-wall. Other areas are less fortunately endowed. In some places history is so sparse that it is a 400-mile drive between memorable spots, which makes the children awfully restless.

There must be politics in this, too. Everybody knows that the South controls Congress, and who thinks that it is a coincidence that the South is loaded down with history, and more of it being made every day? Look at Massachusetts. They've got so much history there that they store the surplus in bins like the wheat in Kansas.

Obviously something needs to be done to make history equally available to all our citizens, without regard to geographical location. Perhaps the Federal Government will have to do it, but I prefer to think that free enterprise can handle the matter efficiently, tastefully and with a nice profit all around.

What I have to offer is the Handy Dandy Historical Shrine Kit. It would come in various models, and in size it would range from the modest (which would require a two-headed calf as an added attraction) to the stupendous, including its own motel and cocktail lounge.

There is no point in going into all the varieties, but perhaps the Famous Personage, Home and/or Birthplace of, Kit Model 16-B will serve an an illustration.

The home itself comes in easy-to-assemble prefabricated sections in a range of regional architectures. Cape Cod and Tidewater Colonial types are included, but I would not expect them to be best sellers, as they have already been rather overdone.

The individual, municipality or civic organization that purchases the Kit would provide a site convenient to major tourist routes and would do the finishing of the interior, adding bullet holes, tomahawk gashes and bloodstains to suit.

Crate "G" contains memorabilia and personal effects of the Personage, such as his spectacles, bill from his tailor, note to (or from) Rutherford B. Hayes, tintype as a small boy, family tree, election posters, army discharge, swords, cane, dentures, lock of hair, set of fifteen favorite books, goosequill pen, pressed rose from Legendary Lost Love, cufflinks and wife's bustle.

That is the basic set. A smaller crate "K" provides specialized items depending on whether the Personage is to be military, literary or political—extra weapons and uniforms for the first, for example, inkwells and desk for the second, and campaign buttons for the third.

Each exhibit comes with its own little card which describes the item and contains some such phrase as "said to be," "attributed to," and so on. There is always an off chance that somebody who claims to be a historian will wander in and start arguing about authenticity, and these phrases will let the proprietor off the hook. If such persons persist in causing a disturbance they should be ushered out the door and their fifty cents refunded. They would, however, be charged fifty cents for the bumper sticker, which has already been affixed to their car and which is free to less nosy visitors.

Anyway, the covers of the exhibition cases will be made out of our special glass with built-in dirt so that nobody will be able to see any of this stuff very clearly.

The Kit includes a good supply of roadside signs reading "Blank Miles to Original Home of Insert Name." Purchasers of the Kit are reminded that they must think up a name and put it on each sign. If everybody just left the signs the way they are, with the reference to the Home of Insert Name, the tourist would naturally be confused and history would suffer.

All Kit customers would be expected to provide a good historical name, such as Endicott TraversEròd, and register it with the company to avoid duplications.

Oh, yes, the Kit also has a guest register, half full of signatures of people from all over the world. Nothing comforts the tourist like knowing that a lot of other people have paid their fifty cents. Otherwise he is likely to stop and wonder who Endicott Traverserod was and why he should pay fifty cents to see his dentures and his wife's bustle.

THE VIEW FROM THE BACK SEAT . . .

Sir:

There is a lot written in the newspapers about how much trouble it is traveling with children. This is because, although being only eight years old, I know that the communications media are in the hands of Them, meaning the Grown-ups, so naturally it is their side of the story that gets the big headlines splashed across the front page.

Little kids never get a break in the media. Like they will probably say that this letter wasn't written by an eight-year-old boy because it isn't full of misspelled words and funny sayings. Misspelled words and funny sayings are what grown-ups think that eight-year-olds put in their letters. Eight-year-olds, on the other hand, have too much respect for the integrity of the medium.

The point of this communication is that people who say "Have you ever traveled with children? Hoo! Ha! What a headache!" ought to look at it from the angle that it's not exactly a picnic traveling with parents.

I'm going to have to ask you to withold my name for Obvious Reasons, because some of this is sort of personal, but you travel with parents and you stop to visit an aunt and/or uncle, some of those vague people who have cheeks you have to kiss. They will say to your father, "How's the trip going, Sam?"

And he, your very own father, will say, "Well, Robert Benchley said there were two ways to travel, first class and with children."

Everybody breaks up over it.

I call it a rude remark to make in front of children, eight years old or not.

If a relative would ask me how I liked the trip and I said "Well, as Sheldon Grogan says, there are two ways to travel, first class and with parents," there wouldn't be laughing.

There would be cries of "No television for you, young man," and "Who is Sheldon Grogan?" I never ask them who is Robert Benchley.

You won't believe this, unless you are a parent, but one time my father said to me, "No more rocks, Charlie. Every time we stop you pick up a souvenir rock. We got a carful."

On the same trip my mother had picked up two iron pots to make soap in and a spinning wheel. What's the use? If a kid expects to see any television at all, he can't ask why some people are allowed to pick up crummy old pots and spinning wheels and other people can't have a few rocks to keep them company in the back seat.

Which reminds me that parents will often tell the siblings in the back seat to quit that fighting. Most back-seat fights aren't anything more than a little elbow-nudging and finger-twisting. You ought to hear what goes on in the front seat. But no kid dares yell, "O.K. No television for you people in the front seat unless you cut out that fighting."

Traveling with children may not be first class, but traveling with parents is steerage.

✳✳✳✳

A SKIRMISH WITH SCIENCE

*Or: What's a nice computer like you
doing in a place like this?*

✳✳✳✳

If there is one segment of our society which needs an Advancement Association or an Anti-Defamation League it is the machine. In almost any gathering you will hear the rap being put on the computer that figures out the department-store bill, scans the income tax or answers the telephone.

In more primitive days, people thought it was funny to joke about ethnic minorities, making sport of their gaucheries, real or fancied. We have outgrown that sort of thing.

But we seem to have no compunction about spreading gossip and retelling third-hand anecdotes intended to ridicule machines or cast aspersions on their intelligence. When a computer writes a clerk's pay check for eight million dollars we put it on the front page and laugh in that irritating, superior way we have and say, "Well, after all, isn't that typical of a machine?"

Of course, as in the case of bigotry of all kinds, this attitude toward our electronic friends is rooted in fear. We are afraid of economic competition, of demands for social equality, of the threat which the machine seems to pose to our long accepted way of doing things.

The machine is a particularly vulnerable target because, except in the farther reaches of science fiction, it can't answer back. It knows only what we have fed into it, and you may be sure we have programmed it for docile servility.

I am afraid that some of this anti-machine hysteria may have crept into this chapter. As a child of my time I share the very prejudices I deplore.

However, comments on the computer, automation and the recorded message have been held to a minimum in order to provide a somewhat wider view of the wonderful world of science and technology.

⚹ Computers now do most of the planning for our wars. It would seem only fair to let them do the fighting, too.

I HEAR AMERICA SINGING, PRERECORDED . . .

"Hello, Sutforth's Dry Goods?"

"This is Sutforth's Dry Goods, your wish our command. This is a recording. When you hear the tone please wait one second then place your order. (*Blap, followed by several seconds of silence*) Thank you for calling Sutforth's. This is a recording."

"Will you say that again please?"

"This is Sutforth's Dry Goods, your wish our command. This is a recording. When you hear the tone please wait one second then place your order. (*Blap, followed by several seconds of silence*) Thank you for calling Sutforth's. This is a recording."

"You're not a recording. It sounded different this time. Instead of saying, 'This *is* Sutforth's' with the emphasis on the *is*, the second time you emphasized the *this*."

"This is Sutforth's Dry Goods, your wish our command. This is a recording—"

"You are not a recording. I ought to know a recording when I hear one; it's all I listen to all day. You are a real, live person."

"This is Sutforth's—"

"Shut up. (*Aside*) Hey, Francine, come listen to this. I've got a real, live person on the telephone. I am not kidding. It is not another one of my jokes. Listen to this—"

"This is Sutforth's Dry Goods, your wish our command. This is a recording. When you hear the tone please wait one second then place your order. (*Blap, followed by several seconds of silence*) Thank you for calling Sutforth's. This is a recording."

"You are a person. A human being with dandruff and gallstones and who knows what all, like everybody else. I can hear you breathing. (*Aside*) Couldn't you hear the breathing? What do you mean you're not sure. It was huh-huh-huh. Breathing, like I haven't heard on a telephone in five years. I tell you there is a human hand holding that phone. Listen again."

"This is Sutforth's Dry Goods, your wish our command. This a recording. When you hear the tone please wait one second then place your order. (*Blap, followed by several seconds of silence*) Thank you for calling Sutforth's. This is a recording."

"You sneak, why are you saying you are a recording when you aren't? (*Aside*) Didn't you catch it that time?"

"This is Sutforth's Dry Goods—"

"I know you. You're old man Sutforth and you're drunk. Or you're too cheap to fix your recorder. What's the matter with you, Sutforth? (*Aside*) What do you mean it doesn't sound like old man Sutforth? I go bowling with him every week and he breathes just that way—huh-huh-huh."

"This is Sutforth's—"

"Cut it out, Sutforth. If I wanted to talk to you I'd see you at the bowling alley. When I call a place of business I want to talk to a recording, not some old nut who can't even bowl."

"This is Sutforth's Dry Goods, your wish our command. This is a recording—"

"Sutforth, for the last time. My wish is that you'd admit you are there pretending to be a recording for some diabolical reason I don't even want to know about. Speak up like a man."

"Thank you for calling Sutforth's. This a recording."

"All right, Mr. Smarty-Maniac Sutforth, you've gone too far this time."

CLICK.

"Hello, police department? I want to report a fiendish scheme by old man Sutforth, trying to drive me as batty as he is by pretending to be a recording. Get over there right away with the searchlights and the bullhorn and yell, 'O.K., Sutforth, we know you're in there, come on out!' "

"This is your police department. This is a recording. When you hear the tone state the nature of your complaint. This is a recording."

"Clancy? Sergeant Clancy. That's you. I can hear you breathing. Pretending to be a recording. It's a plot to unhinge my mind. Real people answering telephones. (*Aside*) Call the psychiatrist. You already have? What did he say? A recording answered? You fool. It wasn't a recording. It was the doctor pretending to be a recording."

CLICK.

"Lie down? A cool cloth? The green-and-white capsule? Thank you, dear."

AN EYEBALL-TONSIL CONFRONTATION . . .

For years now, science has been hacking around about giving us a telephone system by which we can see the person we are talking to. And there has been levity and low laughter.

People have said, "Tee-hee, what if you were getting out of the shower?" Well, the bathrobe is within the reach of most of us.

I don't like this sniggering downrating of what could be one of mankind's greatest boons.

Critics have brought forward the theory that this invention would ruin the free day off at home. They say, "If you call down at the plant and tell Mr. Whomever that you are in bed with a bug he's going to have to take your word for it. But if he can see you he will say that you look extremely spry to him and either get down to work or pick up your time at the end of the week."

These critics are spoofing. The way I visualize it is that you call in and say you are sick. Mr. Whomever replies that you don't look sick. You aim the mouthpiece down your throat and say, "Just take a look down there, Sam."

Here's a guy on the other end of the wire looking down your throat. Sick or well, the inside of a man's throat doesn't look exactly great. In the first place, as Dr. Krankheit once remarked, it's dark down there. Eerie and spooky.

"Yeah," he'll say, "you look like one sick boy."

"Would you like to look in my ear, Sam?" you ask. He begs off.

Rather than posing a threat to absenteeism, the see-whilst-talking telephone will open new vistas as far as shirking work is concerned.

WHY NOT GIVE MACHINES THE VOTE?

My feeling about automation is that it gets the machines off the street corners and out of the taverns and gives them useful work to do.

One of the first machines I remember was one where you put in a penny and a little monkey would turn around and deliver you a piece of chewing gum. I thought it was fine but my father said that a machine like that would never amount to anything, and he was rude to that machine. Especially when it didn't give the piece of chewing gum, as it often didn't. I used to think this was inefficiency, but what it really was was that the machine's feelings were hurt.

Machines for too long have been given the menial jobs to do—waxing the floors, vending the cigarettes, making the ice cubes, mixing the drinks, driving people from here to there. And a lot of these jobs have put machines into bad environments and situations where there was no stimulus to get ahead.

How often have we seen a machine in a lunch-room, playing records, flashing lights on and off, making a fool of itself. And we have said, "It's a shame, nice, bright machine like that with all the personality in the world and a sophisticated circuit system, wasting its time in a place like this."

We have prided ourselves on our machine relations in this country and said that machines were happy and useful as long as they knew their place. But the naked fact was that no machine could hope to get an executive position or be in a place where it could make decisions.

Now this is all changing. The machines are moving into the centers of power, and it is a bitter pill for some people to swallow.

They can't accept the idea that they may have to go to a

machine for an opinion or to get their expense accounts approved. These people are living in the past.

The day of prejudice in employment is over. A computer that can compute the best gets the job whether it is made out of steel or flesh and blood. It is a development which had to come. Machines couldn't be kept down forever.

I have a friend who went home the other night and told his wife, "You know, when they first said I was going to be working next to a computer I didn't like the idea. I'm afraid I had made a prejudgment. I thought all machines were pushy and noisy and when you let one in why it would bring all its friends.

"But this computer I am working next to is one of the dandiest fellows we've ever had around the shop. He's quiet, minds his own business and doesn't bum cigarettes. If anything is wrong with him he just blinks a red light instead of going into a long story about how he strained his back moving the piano over at his brother-in-law's house. After work he doesn't want to stop and have a couple of beers to tell me about his problems at home. I just unplug him, cover him with a plastic sheet, and that's all there is to it.

"Of course I know that he is being mentioned for the vice-presidency that you and I had always thought I'd get some day, but I don't mind. At least his wife won't be showing up in an ermine coat at the company party just to rub it in about your dyed squirrel.

"I notice I keep saying 'he' because he's such a regular fellow. Maybe it should be 'she,' but with a machine it doesn't make any difference, which is another aid to efficiency around the place."

So I think, instead of getting panicky, we ought to realize that the machines are only getting, at long last, what has always been their due.

We're all in this thing together.

✳ If a couple are introduced by an electronic matchmaker, do they have to ask the comupter to be best man at the wedding?

WHEN WE WERE YOUNG, LASS, AND ALL THE WORLD WAS
BLACK AND WHITE . . .

I have a friend, a young friend, who is enjoying a moment of glory which I hardly have the heart to tell him will be brief, but I will anyway. He might as well know it.

He is an expert adjuster of color-television sets, and as these machines are filtering down to middle-income brackets and below, he is in very large social demand.

He makes night calls, even on Sunday. There will be a desperate ring on his telephone. A harassed housewife gasps, "Ed Sullivan is blue and Sam is kicking the set."

Already my friend is fumbling into his coat, his hat brim in his teeth, as he mumbles, "Tell Sam to take two aspirins and lie down."

"Can you come right away?" implores the housewife. "Ed Sullivan is getting bluer and, Great Arthur Godfrey, you ought to see what color Leslie Uggams is coming out. And there's only twelve minutes left of the whole show."

"Calmness is all," says my friend. "Boil lots of water. I'm on my way."

I should make it clear that my friend is not a television repairman. It is just that he knows how to twiddle the controls so as to return Ed Sullivan to his genial Irish hue and take the general purplish cast away from Miss Uggams.

When he arrives at the scene of the disaster, he makes a few simple manipulations and says, "There you are. Keep Sam away from the set. Don't anybody touch anything."

"What should I do with the boiling water?" asks the housewife.

"Pour it out," says my friend. "It was just to keep you busy until help arrived."

"Bless you," says the housewife.

"I am as close as your telephone," responds my friend. He is very modest about his skills.

"It is merely a certain sensitivity of touch," he says. "Plus a little technical knowledge, such as knowing what color Lawrence Welk is supposed to be. A lot of people don't know that, and it makes it difficult for them to adjust the set. But mainly, I would say, it is raw courage. Many laymen are so frightened of their color TV that they approach it timidly instead of showing it, straight off, who is master."

He may find it hard to believe that his day of importance is a transitory thing, but that is what it is.

I have seen experts of this kind have their moment of celebrity and then fade back among the anonymous crowd. It was thus in the early days of black-and-white TV. For weeks, maybe even months, there was a great demand for the man who knew the difference between the Vertical and Horizontal knobs, how to cure flop-over and when to jiggle the rabbit ears.

Most of us were so awed by the miracle of little pictures being wafted into our living room that we were afraid to touch any of the array of switches.

Even the Off button was treated in those days with a respect bordering on reverence which it lacks in these more sophisticated times, when even the youngest child is assumed to be able to cope with such esoteric controls as Brightness and Contrast.

Before that, older folks may remember when Ed Mumford had to be summoned from next door to turn the dials on the superheterodyne, a monster of electronic ingenuity, which no one except Father was allowed to touch, and he only tried it when Ed was not available. Ed was a man who could get Pittsburgh on his crystal set and was, therefore, regarded as a genius in the area of radio.

His skills become decreasingly in demand, and he himself was one of the last to face up to the problems of television, sitting helplessly in front of blurred and distorted images until an expert of a newer generation came along.

So I say to my young friend: Enjoy while you can the hot white light of fame which beats upon you as the man who understands color TV, for these laurels wither quickly. Try not to let your memories be bitter.

✳ The teacher tells the little boy down the block that the world is round, but he's been watching it on television all his life and he knows it's rectangular.

GREAT, DRIVING BLIZZARDS OF HAPPINESS AND TORRENTIAL GUSH . . .

A few years ago when the weather bureau started issuing something it called the Discomfort Index, which combined heat and humidity in a formula to give us the official word as to how we were enjoying the summer, there were civic protests. Many communities preferred to think of it as a Comfort Index, as having a more positive ring to it.

Why can't we have more of this attitude at other times of the year? We get these forecasts that are designed to make the approaching weather sound terrible. This country, let us remind ourselves, was not built by people who thought tomorrow was going to be punk. It was built by people who had the optimistic faith that tomorrow would, somehow, be better.

It didn't turn out that way too often, but the thing to remember is the optimism, the rejection of negative thinking.

What we have now is the weather bureau telling us, in effect, "Folks, there is a terrible, fierce blizzard on the way and you're going to hate it."

How much pleasanter it would be if we would rephrase it something like this:

"Guess what, folks! When you wake up in the morning and look out the window you will be greeted by a veritable fairyland of white. The lovely virginal snow, which comes highly recommended to us by leading poets, will transform streets and highways from their customary dullness into winter wonderlands. And best of all, this beauty will accumulate to a depth of eight generous inches."

That is the kind of forecast that would make us look forward eagerly to the next morning and we would spring from our beds to see if it had truly happened, instead of dragging ourselves out to groan "Oh, no" at the sight of the way the family sedan at the curb is just a bump in the snowscape.

The police and highway patrol tell us to stay home when there is ice and snow on the roads, which may be a good idea, but they emphasize the scary element by pointing out that we may slide into a ditch or some other unpleasantness.

It would be better, psychologically speaking, if we were advised along these lines:

"Here's a great idea, friends! Why not telephone the shop that you won't be in today and stay home and have one of those simply great family days, with corn-popping and parcheesi or maybe taking from the shelf some well-loved old book and reading aloud to the kiddies? Just think how lucky we are to be living in a climate where once in a while we get an opportunity for a rousing experience such as this.

"Or if you feel you simply have to get out on the roads,

there are going to be some really outstanding chances to meet some fine new friends. The people who man the nation's tow trucks, for example, are among the greatest folks you'll ever want to meet. When they eventually get to you, chances are you'll find that they are warmhearted and with a smile for one and all.

"Driving today has practically a surefire guarantee that you will meet some of these splendid folks, to say nothing of snowplow crews and maybe a helicopter pilot if you have to be plucked from a drift.

"Another dividend from the condition of the roads is that the odds are excellent that you will be hopelessly marooned about a mile from the nearest habitation. If you make it to the farmhouse, you are likely to meet the wonderful family that lives there and you will be invited in for a bowl of hot soup, if their electricity happens to be working."

Communities with this kind of weather need to learn to treat it as an asset instead of taking it with so much grimness.

People can learn to enjoy almost anything, once they're persuaded that the official line is that it's supposed to be fun.

RUN NEXT DOOR, DEAR, AND BORROW A CUPFUL OF
MEMORIES . . .

Scientists (to be specific, a group of psychologists at UCLA) are having good results in transferring memory from the brain of one rat to that of another.

Earlier they had been similarly successful with flatworms, although it is hard to think of exactly what a flatworm would have to remember.

The scientific mind, as you well know, does not engage in

fanciful speculations based on limited laboratory experience, but the sensation-seeking columnist is under no such professional restriction.

So the way it looks to me is that we are on the threshold of something really big. If transferring ribonucleic acid (excellent stuff) from one rat's brain to another also transfers the first rat's recollections of how to run mazes, etc., who is to say it wouldn't work with humans?

As a matter of fact, I have long suspected that something of this nature was already taking place. Otherwise how are we to explain the kid sportswriter's memories of Honus Wagner or the twenty-two-year-old dramatic critic's total recall in relation to Sarah Bernhardt or Duse? The indications are clear that they have been mainlining ribonucleic acid from some older generation.

There has been some speculation that the educational process of the future will be by hypodermic needle. If you're having trouble with your calculus, a little shot of Essence of Einstein will save you the trouble of further study.

One hitch in this concept seems to be that the newly injected memory tends to fade. Thus the man with a whiff of Einstein could go great for a few weeks, then wake up some morning with nothing more mathematical in his mind than the odds on today's ball games.

This very element, the fact that the memories do not persist for any extended length of time, strikes me as the most intriguing part of the whole idea.

What I envision is a library of other people's memories. We might as well face it—most of us ordinary people are too busy to live really exciting lives. Now the doctors are tacking about twenty years on the end when we will have nothing much to do except sit around with our memories.

We can remember the time we almost took a job in Des Moines, or in what year which kid had his teeth straightened, or the name of the musician who played the mighty Wurlitzer at the old Bijou, or the trip where we had the flat tire in Hoisington, Kan., or the time we saw Milton Sills and failed to get his autograph, or the night the electricity was off for an hour, or the summer when it was over a hundred for eight days straight.

Now these are good, serviceable memories, but you can remember them all in about five minutes, and twenty years of rerunning them will get a little monotonous, especially since you and your wife have the same memories and there is nothing you can remember that she doesn't know (if you are the decent chap I take you to be) and vice versa.

Under my plan, you would go to the memory library and take an injection of, let's say, Errol Flynn's memories, if you were in that kind of mood. At the same time your wife could get about two weeks' worth of Mme. Curie's recollections. I am choosing the names at random merely to indicate the scope. Think of the fascinating times you could have sitting by the fire, exchanging remembrances of things past.

After these shots wear off you could take on the memories of Ernest Hemingway or Bobo Newsom or Everett Dirksen and your wife could remember being Marilyn Monroe or Pavlova or Lillian Russell.

It seems ridiculous for us to settle for our own rather tepid memories when science has it in its power to let us remember being Babe Ruth or Jack Dempsey.

STOCK YOUR FREEZER WITH TALENT . . .

Several comic-strip artists and other scientists are becoming interested in the subject of suspended animation or human hibernation. The challenge is that if people could be frozen, or somehow put into a deep sleep, various benefits would ensue.

Take a football coach, for example, who recognizes that a good T-formation quarterback doesn't come along every year. Suddenly he finds himself with two T-formation quarterbacks. The way it is now, one of them will go to waste or transfer to another school. Think how handy it would be if the lad could be quick-frozen and kept on ice until the other ace graduates.

Imagine the drama when an injury required an unexpected replacement in the Great Big Annual Traditional Classic. "Get over to the locker," the coach would snap to one of the assistant managers, "and thaw out O'Shaughnessy."

Or let's take politics. How often do we say, "Ira P. Insight could be a great statesman but he is twenty-five years ahead of his time"?

As soon as this suspended animation thing is perfected, we could tuck Ira away for twenty-five years, at which date, presumably, he and the times would be in joint. (It would, of course, be necessary to leave some kind of note so that Ira wouldn't get lost. People might forget where he was, and we would have gone to all that trouble for nothing.)

Suppose a man makes a game run at the Presidency, but loses by the narrowest of margins, which means that a lot of people thought that he was the best man for the job. He is knocked out of contention for four years, and probably eight. The mathematics of the thing may be such that by the time he had another chance he would be too old.

His supporters could stash him away for eight years, at which time he could be revivified at the same age as when he went to sleep.

There would be another great advantage here in that while he is cooling it he would not be likely to make any mistakes.

He would deliver no unfortunate speeches, engage in no ill-advised debates, avoid questionable associates and write no books that would irritate anybody.

AFTER THE MOON, THE DISCOVERY OF HUMAN NATURE
ON EARTH . . .

I am as eager as nearly anybody for us to get to the moon and find out all the keen information that's up there waiting for us. But I want to warn my scientist buddies that the minute they set a safe foot on the lunar surface everybody will give a sigh of relief and then lapse into what I call the if-you-why-can't-you syndrome.

For the benefit of any who may be unfamiliar with the principle of if-you-why-can't-you, I shall point out the way in which it will be used in the event of a journey to the moon.

Scientists will hear from many people.

Humanitarians: "If you can put a man on the moon, why can't you put an end to war in this world?"

Educators: "If you can go to the moon, why can't you raise teachers' salaries?"

Aesthetes: "If you can send an expedition to the moon, why can't you get the beer cans off the side of the road?"

Sneezers: "If you can solve the technical problems of a lunar voyage, why can't you solve the problem of the common cold?"

And so, scientist buddies, it will go. Everyone with any special interest, laudable or not, will want to know why, if you can get to the moon, you can't do something else.

It's a streak that runs though the human character like fat

in bacon. Moon travel will, I predict, bring it out in a rather exaggerated form, but it is all about us.

And while many of us will be asking these questions of the scientists, demanding to know why, if they can get to the moon they can't pave our street, desalt our water or unpollute our air, we will also have some sympathy for them, or at least we should have. Because very few of us are immune to if-you-why-can't-you.

Let us say that you are an executive-type businessman. Your wife will be likely to say, "If you can send a fleet of trucks up to move a great big factory from Trenton, N.J., why can't you get one little old truck to move Hazel June's Brownie pack to camp?"

Or an employer will remark, "If you can roll 185 in the bowling league why can't you get around and call on the customers more than once a month?"

Husbands have been known to say, "If you can earn a degree from the State U. with a major in mathematics, why can't you cook a steak that doesn't have to be chopped with an ax?"

I hope I have clarified the essential nature of if-you-why-can't-you. The classic formula calls for opening on a complimentary note: "If you can go to the moon—" then snapping the trap with something derogatory and, if possible, wholly unrelated—" why can't you make a zipper that doesn't stick?"

We inflict this business on our children too:

"If you can make Eagle Scout why can't you straighten up your room?"

"If you can get an 'A' in English why can't you take your cousin Norene to the dance?"

"If you can play 'The Scarf Dance' on the piano, why can't you eat your spinach?"

I will leave to deeper thinkers than I the necessary psychic probing to explain why we do this to others, and why they do it to us. I merely want to be sure that the moon scientists are aware of what lies ahead of them.

I'm warning them, they'll be hearing: "If you can go to the moon why can't you develop an automobile clock that runs?"

And, come to think of it, if they can, why can't they?

AMBUSHED AT CULTURE GULCH

Or: Some fallout from the intellectual explosion

✳✳✳✳

The free-form cloud of the culture explosion looms over our society as inescapably as the mushroom of the Big Bomb. There was a time when a man could get elected to Congress merely by alleging that his opponent had a Modigliani in his home, a statement which inspired a lot of rib-nudging and knowing glances. Candidates for mayor won acclaim by pointing out that several holes in the streets could be filled for less than it cost to subsidize an ophicleide player in the municipal band.

But now the swing is the other way, and politicians do not hold their hats in front of their faces to shield them from the photographers when exiting the opera or an art gallery.

Every community yearns for a culture center, which would concentrate all the stuff in one place instead of having it scattered untidily around town.

We are setting our sights high, but the question of money keeps arising. Many years ago a Missouri political figure observed, "Art is on the bum in Kansas City."

This was interpreted as meaning that Kansas City had bum art. My own guess is that it meant art was on the bum in the

sense of looking for a handout to relieve its desperate financial straits.

If so, nothing much has changed. Not long ago the Rocke-
feller Brothers Fund put out a report that the performing arts
are on the bum in America and that culture needs a crash
program if it is going to amount to anything.

Naturally, when a big national problem faces us we must
all come up with either money or ideas, whichever we have
more of. In my case it is ideas, and even then it's only one
idea. But it is a good one..

What culture needs is a spring training camp, or not necessarily spring, but some season of the year when the public
prints and barbershop conversation will be full of how some
rookie oboe player looks like the greatest phenom in the field
since George B. Oglethorpe.

To be quite frank about it, the only thing that makes baseball the thing that hangs the country up the most is the spring
training camps. After the season gets underway it becomes
something of a bore. But the public has been so hopped up by
reading what comes out of Florida or Arizona that it turns out
in great numbers to see these wonders with its own eyes, and
there is enough interest to last, in some cases, for the whole
season and in others, at least through June.

Suppose, before the opening of the big art shows, we were
to read stimulating items such as this:

"Fred Fixative took time out from a busy practice session
today to tell your reporter that he confidently expects to make
a comeback after his disastrous 1966 season. He set the art
world aflame in 1965, his first year in the big time, by his
technique of standing 90 feet away and throwing the paint at
the canvas.

" 'Last year was a nightmare,' said the personable young
abstractionist. 'But the skipper worked with me all winter.
We looked at movies which showed I was raising my left foot
too far before releasing the pigment. I tightened up and, as a

result, lost my control so that at times I missed the canvas entirely. I have changed my stance and this year feel that I am more of a pitcher than a thrower. Also, on the skipper's advice, I am working in a little closer now and using larger canvases.'

"The art writers who have been saying that this slim chap with the boyish grin had lost his stuff may be in for a few surprises."

Well, this would whet our artistic zest, unless I am very much mistaken or unless art fans are different from baseball fans.

Some other possible items out of the cultural training camps:

"Hjalmar Boing, ace tenor of the Fort Worth Mets, resents the tag of good-sing, no-act which has been hung upon him by the opera scribes. He is working on a variety of expressions and now has three: grim, lovestruck, and nauseated, plus a forth which has not yet been perfected but which he refers to as 'my nothing look.' "

"A pulled tendon prevented Fyodor O'Brien, nifty fouetté specialist of the Cleveland Ballet, from taking jumping practice today, but the skipper said admiringly, 'The kid won't stay sidelined for long. He has tremendous desire.' "

"Word from Florida is that Alfred Anapest, popular local poet, is sending pentameters to all sections of the park and is being described by veteran observers as a second Robert Frost. 'The kid has all the tools,' a member of the press corps said, 'and should make it big.' "

"A big year for herself is being predicted by Clarabelle Clang, crowd-pleasing cymbalist for the Boston Orks. Critical fans in culture-conscious Beantown booed the petite miss several times last season, and she admits she wasn't at the top of her form. Without making any alibis, the classy competitor pointed out, 'Last year we played a lot of quiet music that kept me sitting on the bench during most of the concerts.

This year, the skipper has promised to use me more and is even penciling some cymbal crashes into the scores. I need to play every day."

Would this approach work for culture? How do we know unless we give it a try? The click of the turnstiles demonstrates that it has done wonders for professional sports.

How about that, culture fans?

A FIREMAN TO FAN THE FLAME OF GENIUS . . .

A friend thinks that the writer is treated unfairly because, unlike the baseball pitcher, he doesn't have a bullpen behind him.

The writer, he explains, may sail along through the early paragraphs, retiring the side in order, when he suddenly loses his real good stuff. His participles dangle, he incautiously mixes a metaphor, he throws a cliché into the dirt, and before he knows it he is tossing wild syllogisms all over the park.

"As for example, the other day," he said, "I opened the fifth paragraph with, 'The irony of the situation is—' and there I was stuck. I realized I had no idea what the irony of the situation was.

"What I needed was to have somebody stroll in and inherit the situation. Maybe Walter Lippmann. If anybody could be relied on to know what the irony of the situation was, it would have to be Walter Lippmann.

"Like the pitcher, the writer should have, in back of him, a long-reliever and a short-reliever. The long-reliever would come in on those days when a man knows before he has finished the first page that his verbs have no snap to them and his adjectives aren't breaking. He'd be able to take over and go the route.

"The short-reliever, it seems to me, would be of particular

use to the poet. Lots of us have seen a poet coast through the opening octets like the ode was going to be a laugher. He starts to falter in the next four lines, and by the time he gets to the closing couplet he's blown the poem entirely.

"My idea is that the short man would be rushed in to take over the last two lines. After all, he's fresh; maybe he hasn't rhymed anything in three, four days. He polishes off the poem and gets credit for the save."

⁂ Sophia Loren says she is just a "simple girl." But put together in a complicated manner.

AN OPERA TORN FROM THE WOOF AND TWEET OF THE AMERICAN FABRIC . . .

A cultural trend that we must not allow to pass unnoticed is the writing of operas about folks who are famous in Americana, such as Carry Nation, Baby Doe, Lizzie Borden and others.

My plan is to write a series of operas in this vein, not good ones, of course, as this would be beyond my scope, but at least I would have something on paper and could sue for a cut of the royalties when anybody else produces a work on the subject.

Everybody remembers when Gabby Street caught a baseball dropped from the top of the Washington Monument. I have never been able to find out the name of the man who dropped the ball, and this would give an opportunity for some good *mysterioso* passages in the operatic score.

Perhaps there could be a plot twist in which the person who dropped the ball from the top of the Washington Monument, the one that Gabby Street caught, would turn out to be his long-lost brother, or even his girl friend disguised as a boy (they do a lot of that sort of thing in opera, although the average soprano has a tough time convincing anybody that her real name is Rodolfo, much less Burleigh Grimes).

I am just using this part about long-lost brothers and girl friends as illustrative matter without suggesting that they had any actual role in the real-life happening. There is, after all, literary license.

Anyway, the big scene would be a duet with the fellow who plays Gabby Street (a tenor, I suppose, although it seems inappropriate) standing on the stage singing his lungs out and circling around holding his catcher's mitt in a receptive manner.

Unless this opera is put on in a very tall theater, the baritone (or soprano) who plays the character who drops the ball would have to be out of sight up in the loft, which would make it all the more effective.

Gabby: (*Sings*) Drop the ball.

Voice from Above: (*Sings*) *Buona fortuna* (Lots of luck).

Gabby: (*Sings*) Drop the ball!

Voice from Above: (*Recitative*) Alas, the window she's a-stuck.

I can't really explain the Italian accent of the man in the monument, but it would seem to fairly well rule out Burleigh Grimes.

It occurs to me, too, that there might be a good opera in the debate over the health hazards of cigarettes. After all, there has just been an opera on Carry Nation, and booze figures prominently in a lot that happens on the musical stage.

So far cigarettes have been limited to Carmen who, you will remember as the great golden curtain rises, works in a cigarette factory.

Even a nonmusician can imagine some rich doomful music to be sung by the researchers studying the effects of smoking on the lungs. (Would a chorus of white mice be practical?) And there would be opportunities for excellent coughing scenes. There is no reason why a girl should have to play in *La Boheme* to get a solid coughing role.

Why has no one thought of "Duncan Hines, an Opera in Three Acts"? Think of the opportunities here for a musical mélange. There could be Spanish music when the great culinary investigator visited a Spanish or Mexican restaurant, Swedish with the meatballs, and so on—you get the idea. Comic cooks and waitresses always add a lot to any show and there would be plenty of chances to work them in, also intrigue and suspense over which restaurant gets which rating. Maybe even a poison plot could be included.

I can't think of any American political heroes who have had operas written about them. There was *Fiorello*, of course, but it was not a serious opera of the kind I have in mind. Imagine the drawing power of an opera called "Richard M. Nixon" or "Wayne Morse," to say nothing of "Everett M. Dirksen."

RECOGNITION OVERDUE, AT THREE CENTS A DAY . . .

A man who loves libraries feels he ought to do something for the cause. So what I have done is figure a surefire way to work National Library Week into the conversation. It is to ask, "By the way, does anyone know the first name of the Dewey who invented the decimal system that they use in libraries, especially during National Library Week?"

Some will say George, who was the admiral, or John, who wanted kids to have fun at school, or Tom, who was almost President that time.

All wrong.

"The man," you announce, "whose decimal system is widely used in libraries, especially during National Library Week, was Melvil (only two *l*'s, only one *e*) Dewey."

There will be cries of "Let's hear it for Mel," and "Good old National Library Week," and you will feel that you have done a helpful thing for a good institution.

✳ Real class in intellectual folksong circles is for the troubadour to pick the guitar with his Phi Beta Kappa key.

YOU WANT TO BE PART OF THE GREAT SOCIETY? IT'LL
COST YOU 10 PER CENT . . .

There was a piece in the *Wall Street Journal* the other day about a service they have in California where a company takes over your financial affairs, gives you an allowance, pays your bills, etc. It's not like one of these debt-consolidating loan outfits. These people function in the same way as a business agent or a manager does for folks who are in the big fiscal leagues. But they do it for the middle-income bracket.

I don't know that I would necessarily subscribe to the service, but there is a lot of appeal in having an agent, the way the movie stars do or the authors who write the best-selling dirties.

Think of the advantage around the house. You pay Mel 10 per cent of your income. For this he handles your every move.

Suppose your wife invites you to help wash the dishes. The way it is now, all you can plead is a bad back, a tough day at the office or an allergy to Blunk, the new, new detergent. None of these really works.

If you have an agent, you say, "Sorry, Fiona, but you know that all my commitments have to be booked through Mel Media and Associates; I'll give them a tinkle."

You telephone your agent and outline the offer.

"Mannie, baby," he says, "it's not for you. You're getting

too much exposure in the household bit. You helped with the dishes a month ago and it was good for your image. But you can't go on doing the same thing.

"You've got a great career in that family, sweetheart, but you've got to give it air, room to breathe, you know what I mean?"

"But," you will say, "it's a good cause and I'm getting a lot of pressure."

"Look, baby," says the agent. "Any time you want to wash dishes I can get you in the kitchen of the country club. All right? You trust me? I'd say this. Maybe a big spectacular. Like on Thanksgiving or Christmas, when all her folks are there, then I'd say washing the dishes might not be a bad idea, not bad at all. You could even carry out the garbage. But a Thursday in August? Forget it."

You can then inform your wife that, much as you'd like to do it, you can't. That's what you're paying Mel the 10 per cent for.

Or the Boy Scout committee may come around and ask you to go along on the troop's next overnight hike. Again you check with your agent.

He almost shouts into the telephone, "Why do you talk to these people? That's what I'm here for, baby. I got broad shoulders. Refer these people to me. Give them my silent number. Any hour, day or night. I'll talk to them. But the damage is done this time. You'll have to handle them. Just tell them that your agent is all for the Boy Scouts, but he has booked you into the Lethargy Lane bowling alley that night. Tell them you'd love to go on the hike, but you got an iron-clad contract. That's the night you got to bowl."

It's undemocratic that only the celebrities get to have agents to excuse them from things and to do the unpleasant tasks of life.

Nobody likes to ask for a raise. Actors, actresses and people of that sort don't have to.

Why not something like this? A sharply-dressed individual in white-on-white necktie and three-hundred-dollar suit drops in on your boss.

"I'm Mel Media and I represent one of the brightest kids in your shipping department. Frankly the fee we're getting on this is peanuts, but we believe in this boy. Another five bucks a week, or I'll take him across the street to Allied Manhole Cover. As a matter of fact I've already gotten a few nibbles in that direction."

We might as well face it, that the way things are going, the man without an agent isn't going to be able to hack it in our society.

WITHOUT A SONG YOU CAN'T EMERGE . . .

You know what was funny in the fifth grade forty years ago? You would say you were going to write the national anthem of Siam on the blackboard, and you would tell some dopey kid to sing it to the tune of "America," and you would write: "O Wot Agoo Siam," and when the dopey kid would sing it everybody would break up laughing.

It's no good any more. "O Wot Agoo Thailand" lacks punch.

Just a vagrant breeze from the Long Ago, fanned by the harsh fact that today, with so many nations emerging, there is a great demand for national anthems. And not only that. In addition, we are going to be opening more and more universities, colleges, junior colleges, all sorts of institutions of higher learning, and all in need of an alma mater song.

What we must think about is the establishment by farseeing opportunity-grabbers of a cell of talent to meet this need.

Let us imagine the office of Anthems, Inc. Miss Ivy answers the telephone: "Anthems, Inc. Good morning."

"This is President P. J. Gumdrop," says a voice.

"Are you a country or a university?" Miss Ivy asks.

"I beg your pardon?"

"Look, Prexie," Miss Ivy explains patiently, "it makes a difference. Like suppose you are a university and we think you are a country, it could get confusing. It's happened.

"We wrote this simply great national anthem with a lot in it about death to the enemies of Rhubarbia and freedom from Communist aggression. Well, it turned out that Rhubarbia wasn't a country, it was a new junior college in Oklahoma, and they thought the sentiment was a little extreme for singing at football games. It was not only overly fierce, but most colleges prefer not to have political implications in their songs as it makes a bad impression on the public when the students picket against their own alma mater. So, you see, the first thing we need to know is whether you are a country or a university."

"I'm both," says President P. J. Gumdrop. "Here in East Gambonia we are a new nation but a proud one, and your State Department has given us a university. So we need two songs, one for the country and one for the school."

"Splendid," says Miss Ivy. "We can make you a special price on the two. Particularly if you would like to take over the Rhubarbia reject."

"It might present a problem," says the President, "that part about Communist aggression, because the Russians are giving us a dam and the Red Chinese are underwriting our air force."

"Just a little tinkering with the lyrics," Miss Ivy assures him. "We do it all the time—in fact, we often supply alternate stanzas in case of a sudden political coup."

"Please," says President Gumdrop, "you're spoiling my lunch."

"Let's see now. You want one National Anthem and one

university-level alma mater song," Miss Ivy says. "Do you have a river?"

"Why do you ask?" the President inquires.

"Rivers or lakes, any body of water, are very handy anthem-wise, something like 'Where the Mighty Mump-Lump flows' or 'Far Above Lake Something's waters.' Considered very catchy."

"We don't have a river yet, but the Russians have promised us one as soon as the dam is built."

"What will it be called?" asks Miss Ivy.

" 'The Free Peoples Shaking Off Chains—' "

" 'River,' " supplies Miss Ivy.

"Wait," says the President. "I'm not through yet. '—Chains of Oppression by Evil Gangsters, Foreign Devils and Crypto-Capitalists.' "

" 'River'?"

" 'River.' "

"It may take some doing but we'll work it in," says Miss Ivy. "We'll put a task force right on it and have it in the mail right away."

"Fine," he says. "Send the bill to the U.N."

Miss Ivy starts to hang up, then has another thought.

"Oh, say—" she begins.

"What did you say?" asks the President.

"I said 'Oh, say—' "

"That sounds like a wonderful way to start a national anthem," says the President.

"Frankly," says Miss Ivy, "I don't think it's very catchy, but if it's what you want—"

"Thank you," says President Gumdrop.

✳ As far as censorship goes, isn't it better for our children to learn bad words in a comfortable movie theater than to pick them up on the street?

SEMANTICS ON THE ROCKS . . .

I stopped by a drinking emporium the other day to use the telephone, and while I was waiting for the bartender to give me some change (so I could use the telephone), I heard a drinking man order a martini "straight-up."

"What is a martini straight-up?" I asked the bartender.

"It is a martini," he replied, "in a stemmed glass, made of gin and vermouth without any ice in it."

"I thought that was a martini," I said.

"No," he said, "that is a martini straight-up."

"What happens," I asked, "to the man who orders a martini without the straight-up?"

"He gets it on the rocks."

"With ice in it?"

"Exactly," said the bartender, "and probably made with vodka."

And so the wonderful world of semantics goes through another convolution. For years a man who wanted ice in his martini (and the very idea brought shudders to the martini purist) had to specify "on the rocks." Now, perhaps, he could say, "Hold the straight-up."

In other words, what had once been the ordinary becomes the special and what was once the exotic is now the regular.

Some years ago I entered a hat store (to use the telephone) and while I was waiting for the clerk to change a quarter I heard him say to a customer, "I congratulate you on your choice of this conservative but snappy chapeau which will serve for either business or country wear. Shall I feather it for you?"

Hats in those days came without feathers, just as martinis came without ice.

But today the buyer must request the clerk to defeather it.

Or, I suppose, he could ask for a hat "straight-up" to signify that he wanted it without pinions.

It will be interesting to see if this same transition takes place in the field of ladies' swimwear. For the nonce, as I understand it, a lady must specify that she wants a topless suit by some such phrase as "Hold the bra," or she will get the full set.

But if things proceed as they have in the case of the martini and other areas of concern, it will be only a little while before the lady who wants any coverage above the waist will have to specify that she wants the bathing suit straight-up.

It may never happen, but then many people never thought they'd live to see the day when ice had to be specifically opted out of the martini.

KEEP THE FAITH WITH THE BIRDS, BABY . . .

Sam baby, I'd like to take on the California Condor thing but I don't know if it would be ethical. I'm already handling the Great Whooping Crane, and you know how it is in the public relations business, you've got to watch out for conflicts of interest.

I think I can say, in all candor—that's a pretty funny idea there, which I am just tossing out. Could you get people, the opinion molders, the thought leaders to sign their letters "In all Condor"? It just shows what the Pubrel brain can spark off when it doesn't even try.

If you use the idea, Sam baby, I won't send you a bill, but don't forget where you got it. Right?

In all candor, or Condor, I think you have a fight ahead. It's not like you had a product like the Florida Key deer to save from extinction. People look at a picture of a cute little deer and they say "Aaah." They look at a condor and they say

"Ech!" or "Tie down the Volkswagen before he carries it off."

I'm not knocking the bird, Sam, but it projects badly. You're going to need a top man to handle the account but, as I say, I can't fit it in. Still, I'd like to make a few suggestions, just off the top of my head, you understand, that may be of some help.

We had a swinging motto for the Great Whooping Crane— "Don't Shoot Any Big White Bird"—and it worked. How many people do you run into every day, if you talk to cab drivers and others in all walks of life, who have shot a Great Whooping Crane? Few, if any.

Your Condor, as I grasp your presentation, is a big black bird. There is a chance here, it seems to me, to get some of the goodwill that integration has going for it and make it a dynamic force. Just kicking it around, but maybe something like: "Don't Shoot Any Big Bird, Regardless of Race, Creed or Color."

Another thing that worked for us with the Whooping Crane was that every winter we would ship them down to Aransas Pass, Tex. I wish I could say it was my idea, but it was a bright kid on my staff. He's got his own firm now; why should I tell you his name? Anyway, he thought up Aransas Pass, and as a result, thousands of people all over the country read every item about Whooping Cranes to see whether it comes out in the paper Arkansas Pass. It's kind of a snob thing, like knowing that Big Ben is the name of the bell, not the clock.

You probably can't duplicate this kind of success. But what I would do would be to have the Condors turn up every year in, let's say, Las Vegas, on Frank Sinatra's birthday. This would give you a lot of tie-ins, plus good pix possibilities, with the condors perched on the slot machines.

Sam baby, you know that there are all kinds of show-biz personalities who don't have a disease or a cause to sponsor.

All the best ones have been taken. Here's where, if I were you, I'd move in.

Get a Committee of the Arts and Entertainment to Protect the California Condor. I'd try for the personalities that appeal to the young, like Natalie Wood or Bob Dylan and those people. In the Whooping Crane campaign we aimed at an older segment, and I don't think it would be wise for you to try to switch them.

Make it a Fun Thing not to shoot a California Condor. Maybe you could get some Hollywood nut to have a pet Condor and it could build into something bigger than tiger-skin rugs.

Well, as I say, Sam, I wish I could get my teeth into this thing, because there's something more than the fast buck, you know. I really like birds. Don't laugh. You'll find out. They get through to you.

So I wish you a lot of luck with the Condors, baby, but just one thing—don't let them get in the way of the Whooping Crane or I'll slit your throat, baby.

✳ Our affluence is being blamed for spreading ugliness all around us. Back when we were poor we couldn't afford anything but grass and trees.

LOVED THE JACKET, HATED THE BOOK . . .

Why not a law covering truth in book jackets?

Like here is one that says the book is written with "searing honesty tempered with compassion." In exactly what proportions? How searing is the honesty? And how much compassion? I may be a reader who is allergic to compassion, whose system can only tolerate a certain daily dosage. Suppose I spend $5.95 for this book and find out it is overly compassionate and I break out in some kind of rash?

How can I take the book back when I have already spilled coffee on it? There is no place to complain. If it were a box of Dandy Wheezies that is labeled as containing 6 ounces and I take the Dandy Wheezies out and weigh them and they only come to 5.6 ounces I will get fast action under the truth-in-packaging act.

But suppose the book jacket says it is "crammed full of exciting action on every page" and along about the second chapter I come across a page that tells nothing except that the hero looks out the window and notices the sky is blue while he is telephoning the heroine and gets a busy signal. Lots of books that claim to have exciting action on every page have pages like that. Shouldn't I anyway get back that part of my money that represents pages where nothing happens?

The thing that blows the whistle on the whole dishonest book-jacket business is that a book gets different labels when it moves from hard cover to paperback.

In the first instance it is hailed as "hauntingly evocative" and the style is described as "sensitive." In paperback it is a "violently shocking blockbuster" written with "raw and brutal force."

This is the same book, remember, and one or the other of the jackets has to be lying. While we're on this truth kick to shelter the consumer, let's open the umbrella a little wider.

AND ANOTHER THING, GODIVA DIDN'T MAKE THE RIDE
IN FULL, GLOWING COLOR . . .

The discovery that Queen Elizabeth of England is descended from Lady Godiva has given rise to some lighthearted comment that the times cry aloud for a repeat.

I'm afraid not.

Back in the eleventh century, you will remember, the good lady was horrified at the taxes her husband Leofric, Earl of Mercia and Lord of Coventry, was laying upon the people. He said, O.K., he would ease the burden if she would canter around the town in nothing but her long hair.

One version is that Godiva asked everybody to stay indoors with the shutters closed and everybody did so, except a tailor, yclept Tom, who bored a hole and peeped out and was, for his boldness, struck blind.

It might have worked then, but not now. We couldn't seriously expect TV to leave a story like this alone, could we?

The familiar voice: "This is Walter Cronkite, and the last word from Godiva control is that we are now two hours from launch, and counting. Meanwhile, we might take another look at this mock-up of the horse that Lady Godiva will be riding . . ."

And there would be the man in the trench coat standing in front of the home of Godiva's parents:

"Well, folks, it's a quiet morning here, but you can sense the excitement. Inside the modest castle of Lady Godiva's parents are only a few close friends, plus a man from the tax bureau and a representative of the Luce publications, which have bought exclusive rights to the parents' reactions.

"We do know that the family has had breakfast. The milkman, however, who has sold his story exclusively to *Look,* declines to give his name or say how many bottles he left this morning. One cute little feature you may be interested in is that the neighborhood children have been selling Lady Godiva tee-shirts to the curious bystanders."

A bit of a crisis behind the scenes:

"Hello, Sam? Look we're here at this yclept Tom the Tailor's house and there's an NBC camera in front of the peephole. I told Tom what they told you. He says he's got a check for ten G's and a deal is a deal. He says why should he be introduced from the audience on the Ed Sullivan show when he's been promised a five-minute spot on Johnny Carson? All right. We'll set up on the roof and maybe we can zoom down. Yeah. And he's selling sandwiches for five bucks apiece. Liverwurst."

"Can you see anything, David?"

"No, I can't. I don't know why we have to be going through this ridiculous business anyway. It's a bore. Everybody's seen a white horse. Back to you, Chet."

"Well, the cavalcade is just making the turn. You should be able to pick them up at the top of your screen. There are the police motorcycles, followed by the mayor in the open car and two flatbed trucks with cameramen. I'm afraid you may not be able to see Lady Godiva, but she's in there somewhere."

"This is Walter Cronkite with a little sidelight which you might find amusing. Earl Leofric is not here today. He has gone grouse shooting. At dinner last night he told me he had seen a white horse."

Well, folks, that is about the way it would be if Lady Godiva tried it today, except for the wrap-ups the next day with the Nielsen rating showing that ABC got 90 per cent of the viewing audience by showing an old movie and that many viewers wrote in angrily protesting the preempting of "Batman" and "Lost in Space."

Editorials would hail the ride as a major breakthrough, pointing out, however, that it would have little real effect since a tax reduction at this time would be definitely inflationary.

HAVE YOU LENT ANY GOOD BOOKS LATELY?

It's a very easy matter to go around making nasty jokes about people who borrow books and don't return them, but this is one of the few questions I have ever encountered that has two sides. How about the people who lend books? Nobody ever gives them a rap on the knuckles. Instead, they are universally represented as innocent and long-suffering martyrs.

This may be what many of them are, and yet I don't think they should be considered absolutely blameless in the matter of the nonreturn of borrowed books.

Some of them operate on the ethical level of the loan shark who is so friendly and persuasive and ready to do business that he just about forces the money on the borrower, who may not have particularly wanted it in the first place, and then complains because the repayment is a little tardy.

This has happened to many a man:

"Sam," a friend will say, "have you read this simply great book, *The Last Exit to Philadelphia?*"

"No," Sam replies. "What is it about?"

"Well, of course," says the friend, "the title doesn't mean anything. That is, it's not about the Pennsylvania Turnpike. What it is, really, is kind of hard to explain. You'd have to read it. It's a nonfiction novel, or really an autobiography, although it has nothing to do with the life of the man who wrote the book."

"I don't think I'd like it."

"I'll lend it to you," says the friend. "You can read it on at least three levels. First, it's an absorbing adventure tale with spies, but on another level it's a poetic allegory of the human condition and the alienation and lack of commitment in our affluent society. Third, you can read it for the dirty parts."

"Thanks," says Sam, "but no thanks. I got a whole pile of *National Geographics* home I haven't been through yet."

"It says yes to life."

"I don't think so."

"It's the first major work by the leading literary figure of Upper Volta to be translated into English."

"I don't want it."

"A book for the ages, a masterpiece, written with a rare mixture of brutality and tenderness. These are only a few of the phrases leading reviewers have used."

"I don't have much time to read," says Sam. "Just the paper."

"It has been condemned by both the Russians and the John Birch Society."

"I really don't think so."

"In an amazing tour de force the author has developed a truly new stylistic form, combining the epic poem with the Chinese fortune cookie. I'll lend it to you."

"I appreciate it," says Sam, "but it really doesn't sound like my sort of thing."

"It's everybody's sort of thing," says the friend, growing angry. "Even the Supreme Court thinks it's obscene and the Disney people are making a movie of it with Vanessa Redgrave and Soupy Sales. It's *must* reading. I'll lend it to you."

"Well," says Sam, "if it means that much to you, thanks a lot."

The next day the friend hands him the book—1,149 pages of fine print.

Two days later Sam discovers that it's all over town that he is a literary deadbeat who swipes people's books and doesn't return them.

Within five days the friend telephones and asks if there was some misunderstanding.

"Did you think I *gave* you the book, Sam?" he asks petulantly. "Look up the verb 'borrow' in the dictionary, Sam. If, that is, you can read."

"Friend," says Sam. "You can have the book back but you'll have to come get it at the house. I'm going into the hospital with a hernia I got from lifting the thing. What's the hurry anyway? You've read it."

"Of course I haven't read it," says the friend. "Just the reviews. Who has time to read?"

"Then why the panic to get it back?"

"I got somebody I want to lend it to."

A case history of why book borrowers and book lenders sometimes end up less than friends, and is it always the borrower's fault?

✳✳✳✳

SECRET AGENT IN THE
WAR OF THE GENERATIONS

Or: I was a teenager for the CIA

✳✳✳✳

Nature, if we are to judge by most of what we read and hear, has done a funny (or anyway unique) thing in the matter of human growth.

All other living things, animal or vegetable, seem to grow in a more or less steady progression. A tree, for example, is first a little tree and then gets bigger and older and finally dies. But it is at all times a tree. It is not at one period a stalk of asparagus and at another a petunia. Little elephants grow into big elephants without pausing along the way to be a kangaroo or a tiger. This is not to say that a puppy is the same as an old dog, merely to point out that nobody suggests they are different kinds of animal life.

The caterpillar does not resemble the butterfly, but they get along well with one another, and you do not hear much talk among butterflies which refers to butterflies as "us" and caterpillars as "them," or the other way around.

Only among the human types have we developed radically different species into which we change at a rigidly assigned age.

It used to be assumed that human life was a continuous flow from cradle to grave. The individual changed, of course, in size, appearance and mental competence. He acquired wisdom (or maybe didn't) and lost teeth as he went along.

The changes brought by the years were many, but they were changes marking the growth and development of the same person. Life was thought of as an on-going process. To jiggle the metaphor a bit, we figured that we were in a river where some of the drops of water were a little ahead of us, some were behind us, and so on in both directions. In other words, we were part of a population in which some people were a few months and some many years older or younger. And nobody worried much about it.

But now you are an infant until Pow! you're a pre-teen, then Wham! a teenager, Sock! a young adult, Bam! a middle-ager and Oof! a senior citizen.

Naturally, people have always gone through these stages, but what has happened is that these are no longer people of varying ages, they are completely different species. You can tell this is so because they study one another as though they were some strange breed, fascinating but frightening.

There are learned reports upon today's young in which they seem to be approached not as people of an age we used to be, but as a remote tribe with instincts and emotions, to say nothing of language and customs, as incomprehensible to us as those of the Australian aborigine.

The many writers who analyze and discuss the plight of the teenager, the dilemma of the middle-aged and the problems of the aged don't give me the impression that the teenager thinks he will grow into an adult or the middle-ager that he will grow into an elderly person.

Instead of growing they are suddenly transformed from one into another and have no recollection of their previous state or expectation of what is to come, as though a frog were to become a prince and then a rutabaga (not necessarily in that order).

Well, I suppose all this is sociologically sound, and that there are plights, dilemmas and problems peculiar to each age group. What worries me is that we are encouraged to think of these arbitrarily marked off segments of the population as self-contained, hermetically sealed groups, rather than simply as individuals of various ages.

This attitude leads to the assumption that the generations can no longer communicate with one another. Firmly as I reject the idea, I must sadly confess that many of the essays in the following section strengthen that dismal point of view.

Still, there is optimism here. The pieces that illustrate the inability of one peer group to understand any other are followed by several searching probes into the American home and wife-husband relationships. The heartening message here is that, while communication between generations may be difficult, within the same generation it is just about impossible.

MILLICENT X SHOWS HER MUSCLE . . .

Millicent X, thirteen-year-old leader of GEWGU (Get Even with Grown-ups) was asked at a press conference recently if there had been any backlash as a result of her slogan "Teen Power."

She said that there had better not be. "If they mess around with us," she said, "I will pull out every teenager in the country. We'll hit the bricks. Suppose we were to withdraw our support from the economy. One out of every four businesses, at a conservative estimate, from pizza parlors to record companies, would fold up."

An elderly reporter of twenty-four asked the charismatic

leader for her reactions to what has come to be known as the Bobby Phenomenon.

"I flip over Bobby Phenomenon," she replied demurely, "and have all his records. Grown-ups are always trying to put Bobby Phenomenon down. They're pushing our patience pretty far."

The grizzled newshawk explained that the Bobby Phenomenon he had reference to was the amazing turnout of America's young people to greet Senator Robert F. Kennedy of New York wherever he goes across the nation. So impressed by their enthusiasm has the Senator been that he has jokingly suggested lowering the voting age to fourteen or even ten.

"What's this 'jokingly' business?" Millicent X asked in a menacing voice. "When anybody talks about lowering the voting age to fourteen he may get the attention of the teenager, but he better not do it jokingly."

"You think," she was asked, "that there might be a groundswell of Teeny-boppers for Bobby?"

"I doubt it," Millicent X replied. "We don't trust anybody over sixteen. Frankly, we've had it with politicians who say that they are for the teenager, but it turns out that they are some middle-aged type like Senator Kennedy, practically senile, for goodness' sake. I mean how can somebody like that who was maybe young back in the Olden Times understand the needs and aspiration of today's youth?"

Well, she was told, at least the attention that Bobby Kennedy and other political leaders are paying to young people indicates that her movement is creating interest.

"Who needs interest?" she said. "What we are after is fear, and I think we're getting some. I saw this great television show the other night where all these old people were in a fort out West somewhere and they were saying to one another, 'The youths are coming. Boy, we better look out for those youths. If those youths get hold of you, it's terrible.'"

A twenty-two-year-old blond crone in the press corps said,

"I saw that program, dearie, and those weren't youths they were talking about. They were Utes, an Indian tribe. U–t–e, Ute."

"A matter of semantics!" answered Millicent X. "Spelling is one of the worst ways that grown-ups have of putting young people down. However, I find it of interest that an Indian tribe has stolen our name. Doesn't that mean something to you?"

Well, she was asked, if GEWGU were to take an active role in politics, what would be some of the planks in its platform?

"For one thing," she replied, "we want a program of Juvicare, free medical care for teenagers. Such as Government-subsidized ear-piercing. A lot of parents say things like 'No daughter of mine . . .' You'd be amazed how many times people, especially fathers, start out sentences with 'No daughter of mine . . .'

"Anyway, they say no daughter of theirs is going to have her ears pierced and they won't come up with the little bitty bit of money it takes to pay the doctor. We would definitely want free ear-piercing.

"And then, well, we would want better job opportunities. Like the astronauts. They're all old men. Miss Cornish in Current Events makes us watch the spaceship launchings and all you see is a bunch of old men, about forty, for creep's sake, and who even knows *how* old Walter Cronkite is?"

"You want to send kids to the moon?"

"Yes," said Millicent X firmly.

A murmur which was rather hard to analyze ran through the room.

"The real drag of it is, though," said Millicent X, "if we get into the 1972 Presidential election I won't be involved. The torch must be passed to other hands."

"You mean?" asked an ancient Fred Allen fan in the crowd.

"I'll be seventeen years old," sighed Millicent X.

＊ Just because one Beatle has had his hair cut is no reason to predict a mild winter.

SOMEHOW, SOCIETY FAILED GEORGE . . .

A recently discovered letter to Augustine Washington, Esq., from Bushrod Tuckerman, prominent Colonial psychological consultant:

"Dear Mr. Washington: The case of your son, George, is far from unique. His taking his little hatchet and chopping down your cherry tree is a perfectly reasonable act, from his point of view. He was striking out against society, and more particularly against that adult world which demands that he conform to certain patterns of behavior.

"More than that, of course, he was not chopping down a cherry tree. He was chopping down, if you will forgive me, Mr. Washington, you. Or if not you, personally, the father figure, the image of authority.

"He was saying, in effect, 'Here I am. Master George Washington. Look at me as an individual. Enable me to effectuate my relationship with the world around me.'

"The fault, I am very much afraid, lies with you and Mrs. Washington. Have you put too much emphasis on material things, such as cherry trees? Have you let the cherry tree become the symbol of a world he never made, a world against which he can do nothing else but rebel? Have you somewhere along the line, perhaps inadvertently, conveyed to him the idea that chopping down the cherry tree was 'naughty' or 'not nice'? Have you made something shameful out of a perfectly normal act?

"Is it possible that you have failed the boy?

"There are some rather distressing implications in the account you have sent me of the cherry-tree incident. You say, for example, that you sternly inquired of him as to who had chopped down the cherry tree.

"You are much larger than he is, I should judge. And by the rather bold calligraphy in which you have written me, I can imagine that you spoke in a loud, indeed a frightening, voice.

"This thunderous demand from a large and imposing figure of established command, the Man in Charge, so to speak, must have been traumatic for the child.

"Could not you rather have said, 'George, look at this wonderful cherry wood that has somehow or other come our way. Shall we build something of it? Perhaps we can make a little cabin or a lodge for the red Indians?'

"The approach, you see, would have been to appeal to the creative instincts of which, as I read between the lines of your communication, George seems to have quite a few.

"Instead, you put all the emphasis on his destructive act. He must have felt a failure in father-son communication at this point, and I cannot but feel that this experience may lead to future antisocial behavior, such as standing up in rowboats.

"Well, that is all in the past, but I hope you can see the damage that has been done.

"You tell me that George replied to you, 'Father, I cannot tell a lie. I did it with my little hatchet.'

"You seem to feel that this was an admirable act on the boy's part, and you immediately forgave him on the spot.

"Until Freud comes along we won't really know what muddy waters we are involved in here. My tentative diagnosis is that George knew that he was striking a tender nerve. Children are much deeper than we will know for a couple of hundred years yet, but it occurs to me that the lad knew that you had a need to forgive even deeper than his need to be forgiven. So he appealed to you along these lines.

"The quotation, as you give it, sounds extremely well rehearsed to me. It goes against the grain of what we are beginning to understand about the nature of small boys. Frankly, it worries me more than does the mere chopping down of the (symbolic) tree.

"A course of therapy for you and the boy would be lengthy and expensive, but perhaps worthwhile. Should you choose not to seek professional help, I can only wish you good luck in rearing George.

"I fear, however, that you, and possibly the throne of England itself (Ha! Ha!) may be in for trouble from this lad.

"Yr. Ob't Servant"

AND EVERYBODY SPEAKS HIS OWN LANGUAGE . . .

The family, surfeited with Togetherness, has overreacted and is now running wild in a riot of Apartitude. The ideal family of today has a separate telephone number for the children, even different ones for each child. To say that each member of the family has his own television set is merely to repeat what everybody knows. Some families of four have five teevees, even though they can pick up only two channels.

Everyone sits in front of his own set, eating his own TV dinner and waiting for his own telephone to ring. Each member has his own bank account, his own Charge-a-Plate and, if of driving age, his own car.

Old Doc used to bring the family together. When he made a call, everybody got looked at, sick or well, and they could swap symptoms. Now everybody has his own specialist, from pediatrician to geriatrician. For all I know, the trend may be toward the kids having their own lawyers.

The latest, an article informs me, is a separate house for the teenagers. The old people are already off in an apartment by themselves. A home is not a house any more, it's a whole housing project.

Maybe we ought to revive at least a little of the spirit of Togetherness before it's too late and the family is merely a loose confederation of separate entities or at best (or worst) a Common Market.

THE BRIGHT AND MOLDY WORLD OF CHILDHOOD . . .

Sand-castle molds are now available. With the help of these plastic contrivances, the child, seated on the golden strand beside the white foam of the breaking, hissing surf, may erect a prefab castle with crenellated battlements and soaring towers, and all without any strain on the tiny imagination.

He merely puts the wet sand into the mold, turns it upside down, removes the mold, and there is Camelot, the fair and shining town of Arthur's magic kingdom.

The family gathers on the beach—mother in her big straw hat, Dad in his yatchting cap, the chairs set up, the umbrella in place, as the rallying point for the suntan oil, the lotion, the bug-scat spray, the paperback mysteries, the transistor radio, the spare sunglasses, the beachball, the surfboard, the snorkels, fins and face masks.

Mother settles herself with due attention to which part of her anatomy requires additional toasting. The children scatter for activities suitable to their age—all except the smallest, a sturdy lad of eight, who hangs around the ancestral supply dump.

"Go play," says Dad, who has not driven nine hundred miles at great expense to be stared at by an eight-year-old child, sturdy or not.

"Go build a nice sand castle," says Mother, who has studied

the Child in the Culture of Today and knows one doesn't tell them, "Go play"; one gives them specific Guidance, such as "Go build a nice sand castle."

"I can't," replies the child sturdily.

"In the bright lexicon of this family, young man," says Dad, "there is no such word. There stretches before you an unbroken expanse of sand, reaching from the surging tides of Passamaquoddy to the sun-drenched reptile farms of Key West. You have been brought to it at great expense. Go build a castle out of it."

"I can't," the child persists.

"Why?" asks Mother, perceptively aware that the child is troubled and seeking to get at the heart of the matter. "Why can't you build a nice sand castle?"

"Because," says the child. "My plastic prefab sand-castle molds are all back in my sandpile in Wherever, Indiana, our home town nine hundred miles away. And I can't build a sand castle without them. You wouldn't expect me to play baseball without my little shirt that says Inevitable Insurance Co. on the back, would you, and three grown-ups to umpire and a lighted diamond, would you?"

"Certainly not," says Dad, recoiling in horror at the idea.

"You wouldn't expect me to dance on my little toes just out of the sheer joy and exuberance of being a happy, healthy child in the summer sunshine beside the sea unless I executed the proper grace-and-rhythm steps as taught in the Grace and Rhythm class which I don't even take until next year, would you?" the child asks.

"Of course not," his mother says. "That would not be properly relating yourself to activities suitable for your age."

"It would be unwise," Dad puts in.

"Then," says the child, "it is obvious that I cannot build a sand castle without my plastic prefab sand-castle kit."

"You couldn't," asks Dad, tentatively, "just sort of, well, build a castle with your hands?"

"Of course he couldn't," Mother says. "It might be a non-conforming sand castle."

"It wouldn't look like all the other sand castles," says the child.

"That would never do," Dad agrees. "Go on back to the hotel and watch the teevee."

"And tomorrow," Mother says, "we'll get you a new plastic prefab sand-castle kit and you can make a prefab sand castle . . ."

"Just like the ones I make in my sandpile back home," cries the child gladly as he trots off toward the teevee.

GENERATION-TO-GENERATION BOREDOM . . .

"You poor little tads," this grandfather said the other day. "It wrings my old heart to think of you being deprived of an old-fashioned Fourth of July like we used to have. I suppose you want me to tell you about it?"

"Well," said one of his grandchildren, "I've got a skateboard lesson at four o'clock."

"This won't take long," said this grandfather. "It is the duty of every grandfather to tell about how much better things were when he was a boy so that his grandchildren will feel miserable. I am only doing my duty."

"Thank you, Grandfather," the children chorused, and there were cries of "Tell us about it!" and "Get it over with!"

"First of all," this grandfather said, "we made the ice cream. And we turned the crank and turned the crank and turned the crank."

"It sounds like fun," said one of the boys politely.

"Oh, it was wonderful," the old gentleman said. "And finally we had this wonderful peach ice cream."

"Just a minute," said the little girl with the analytical

mind. "You mean after all that cranking you ended up with nothing but one icky flavor of ice cream?"

"Well, uh, yes, but—"

"Boy," various children said, "that must have been some glorious Fourth all right with no banana-fudge, no coffee-butterscotch, no pistachio-pineapple, no marshmallow-mint, no pickled pecan, no caramel-crunch, no peanut-lime, no . . ."

"We liked peach."

"Of course, Grandfather, peach is nice," said the kids, and nudged one another. "What else did you do?"

"One thing that was about the most fun was we would rent a boat and Father, your great-grandfather, would row us around the lake in Stoddard Park."

"And then what?"

"That was all. He just rowed us around."

"Hey," said one of the boys, "remember last year when we went out in the Smitherbys' ninety-seven-foot cruiser with the two-jillion-horsepower engine and we all took turns on water skis? Up and down the old lake at about a hundred miles an hour? Boy, instead of doing that, I wish we could have been in that good old rowboat, just rowing around, like Grandfather says."

"My father rowed very fast," this grandfather said, somewhat defensively. "Once he rowed so fast his straw hat fell off and floated away. We all laughed."

"Glorious," said one of the children. "What else did you do to kill—er, enjoy the day?"

"There was the fireworks, of course. We'd have a big sack, firecrackers and maybe two or three skyrockets. We'd save up our money and sometimes we'd have two or three dollars' worth."

"I guess the old Fourth isn't what it used to be," one of the little boys sighed. "The Merchants' Association is only going to have a two-and-a-half-hour fireworks show instead of three hours like they had last year."

"One year," this grandfather said, "we had two pinwheels."

"Last year," the more romantic of the girls sighed, "we had Richard and Liz Burton all in fireworks, but this year all they're going to have is a reenactment of a Gemini blast-off."

"The fireworks wasn't all," her grandfather said. "The high point of the whole day was when the Congressman made the speech."

"That sounds neat," cried the children. "Real gear. What did you do, scream?"

"No, we just listened while he told us about the proud heritage of 1776."

"You didn't even picket?" asked the oldest boy. "Here was this speaker giving only one side of the question and you didn't picket or hand out pamphlets or sit down in the middle of the street?"

"No, we sat on folding chairs."

"And listened to the whole speech?"

"Yes," said this grandfather. "That was how the glorious Fourth used to be. Too bad you came along too late."

"It sounds glorious all right, Grandfather," said the kids, most of them keeping a straight face.

NO ORGY UNTIL YOU SAY YOUR PRAYERS, YOUNG MAN . . .

My sympathy goes out to any father of young children in these pre-Christmas days. When I was in that line of endeavor it was a snap to dream up a bit of fantasy for the tiny tots.

All you had to do was tell them what the toys were up to when the lights were out and all the household lay asleep. Raggedy Ann and Raggedy Andy came to life, you know, and did a floppy dance, and the Teddy bear had the nurse doll stitch up the tear in his side so that his stuffing wouldn't come out, and the wooden soldier played his drum, but very softly so as not to awaken anybody.

And before you knew it, the child was off to Blanket Bay with a peaceful smile, and Dad was free to tiptoe out of the room and hear Joe Penner on the radio.

But who could begin to describe what happens in the modern nursery when the magic hours of the night activate the toys?

You tuck the child snugly in bed and it's Christmas-fantasy time.

"Tell me about the toys, Daddy."

"Well, first of all, the monsters all come alive and they slither and crawl and clump all over the floor, which may be why we haven't been able to find the Teddy bear or Raggedy Ann lately. The horrible monsters have eaten them all up, and—"

By this time the child is screaming in terror, unless he is pro-monster, and you have a problem on your hands either way.

And there is no pink-cheeked wooden soldier giving a soft tum-tum-tum on the drum. The soldiers in the up-to-date toy chest don't mess around with musical instruments. They are out to kill and defoliate and set cities on fire. They have bazookas and flame-throwers and hydrogen bombs.

Describing the military action when they come to life would require a combination of Hanson Baldwin and Norman Mailer.

In the old-style fantasy, the little wind-up train would chug around its track, taking the dollies for a ride.

Today the action runs to drag-racing and hot rods, and the only action the toy train sees is when one of the supermodified jalopies tries to beat it to the crossing. Any dolls that get in the way are lucky if they don't get run over.

Then there is the problem of the kind of doll that hangs

out in the nursery these days. When Barbie and Ken and all that bunch come to life they're not going to settle for a dolly teaparty.

They're a swinging bunch of conspicuous consumers who are going to be off surfing or picnicking or doing the watusi at some discothèque. No sign of a chaperon, either, and if Raggedy Ann or somebody like that should try to calm things down she is going to be invited to butt out.

Now I am not one who thinks the fun generation is any worse than many another one, but a description of its activities hardly seems suitable for sending little Curlyhead off to dreamland in the most relaxed manner.

So it must be something of a challenge for young fathers without the when-the-toys-come-alive bit to fall back on.

But maybe these days they just leave it all up to television or LSD.

NEW TRADITIONS ARE BEST . . .

We hear a lot about the culturally deprived segments of society, which means people who don't know what everybody else is talking about, which is pretty much the way I am when it comes to the old family traditions of the holiday season.

One will say to me, "We would all spring out of bed on Christmas morning and holler 'Christmas gift!' and the one who hollered it first had good luck."

And I will say, "What happened to the others? Did they get to go back to bed?"

And the one will say, "No, you big silly. But they wouldn't be as lucky as the one who hollered 'Christmas gift!' the first. It's an old Southern custom."

Looking back on it, our family practice was to hang loose

and play it by ear. Some holidays we would go one way, and some another, and it seemed to me to work out all right.

And yet, I am under this growing pressure to have some traditions I can talk about.

For example, someone will say, "At our house we opened one gift on Christmas Eve, and then the next morning nobody got up until Daddy gave a whonk on the tin horn and we would troop down and dance around the tree for five or ten minutes and then open the other presents."

It makes a man feel out of it, so I have started making up holiday customs.

Like I will say:

"Back on the old plantation we had a regular ritual where we would all leap up on Christmas morning and dash for the bathroom and bang on the door, and whoever was in there would say 'Go away,' and the first person to say 'Go away' had good luck, or at least the best luck available in those days."

Or I will invent another tradition:

"In these days, when so few people seem to have any regard for tradition, when they serve TV dinners to their children on the important holidays, we feel it is vital to keep alive the olden, golden ways. Children need to know that there are some things upon which they can depend in these days of shifting values. You may laugh at it as foolish, but instead of TV dinners or hamburgers, well, we have this old family tradition—we send out for pizzas."

TURNABOUT IS FAIR MISERABLE . . .

Westbrook Normal, well-known average man, asked his wife the other evening how her day had gone.

"Nothing much happened," she replied. "The milkman took me to lunch, and it was kind of late by the time I got home so I decided not to initiate the laundry. It's in the hold basket."

"What is this," said Westbook, "about you and Mr. Stukely and a long lunch hour?"

"We conducted exploratory conversations," said his wife, "in re the weekend milk order. He would like to see me step up to an extra bottle of homogenized and two sour creams."

"For this you had to have lunch?" her husband inquired. "Couldn't you just have marked the card?"

"Of course."

"Then why?"

"Well," said Ethel, "you are always asking me why I don't run this house efficiently the way you run your office. So I've decided to try it, starting today. For example, who did you have lunch with?"

"Luther Whipsnade of Ad Hoc products," replied Westbrook.

"Why did you have lunch with him?"

"Because he is trying to sell me a new one of those little bumpy rubber pads for Miss Snavely to count out the change on in case anybody buys a stamp. We had lunch on it."

"On a little bumpy rubber pad?"

"No, on the whole proposal. We went over it thoroughly and had three martinis and drew pictures on the tablecloth and he got a deductible receipt for tax purposes," snapped Westbrook.

"Just like Mr. Stukely, the milkman, and me," said Ethel, "except for the martinis. Mr. Stukely has an ulcer and I had a small sherry. Often and many a time I have heard you tell me that the wheels of commerce could not grind without the lubrication of the business lunch. So if I am going to run the house like an office, I'm certainy not going to make any purchases without giving it a good, long lunch hour of discussion. Friday, Dianne Lee from the beauty parlor is taking me to lunch to block out preliminary plans for a projected perm."

"Well," said Westbrook. "What's for dinner?"

Ethel handed him a stack of fifty copies of a note, which said, "We are eating out tonight." At the head of it was typed, "Attention all personnel" and "Initial and return" and "Distribution A." At the bottom were letters and figures as follows: "bn-100-r-gl-30-xc."

"What is this?" asked Westbrook Normal.

"I have bought a copying machine," said Ethel, "of the kind that you say is saving hundreds of dollars a week at the office. I mean, like instead of telling Karl Krumfoot that Labor Day is a holiday you make seven hundred and fifty copies and give him one. I don't quite see the point, but if that's the way it is in the business world, that's the way it is here. Please initial and return through proper channels."

"What's all this stuff at the bottom?"

"Who knows?" said Ethel. "But it's cute and looks impressive, don't you think?"

"It does that," said Westbook. "But what is this about eating out tonight?"

"I have closed the kitchen," said Ethel, "since a cost survey shows that it is an uneconomical operation with Kevin away at camp and Sally June visiting your cousins in New Jersey. The mark of an efficient home manager is that she knows when to wrap up a losing operation."

"But I'd rather eat at home," said Westbook.

"Sentiment has no more place in the home than in the office, where, as I have heard you say many a time, especially when you fired my brother, it has no place at all. I am getting out a memo on the subject in the morning, five hundred copies."

"There is more than efficiency, my dear," said Westbook; "there is also the matter of personnel morale. I want a home-cooked dinner tomorrow night."

"I'm afraid not," said Ethel. "I'm thinking of buying a pair of shoes."

"Does that take all day?"

"Well," said Ethel, "Mr. Orbital from the shoestore and I are playing golf tomorrow afternoon. You always say that the place to get business done is—"

"On the golf course," said Westbrook Normal. "I know. And I'm sorry. Now let's get back to running the home like a home."

"Not for a week or so," said Ethel. "I had no idea efficiency could be so much fun."

HOW HIGH THE JINK . . .

This man's wife had been reading the news out of Washington and she asked him, "What are high jinks?"

After fumbling around for a while, he got out the dictionary and reported that jinks are pranks or frolics. Webster, who abjures moral judgments, made no distinction between high and low jinks.

"You mean all this to-do is because of pranking and frolicking?" she said. "It's disappointing. It sounded like something daringly sophisticated, but apparently it's more like some fat man dancing around with a lampshade on his head or maybe people squirting other people with seltzer. I can't see much of a security risk in that. Can you imagine some important lobbyist inviting a Senator out for pranks and frolics?"

"Perhaps," he said, "but I'd have to work on it."

"People, particularly the news media," she said, "should be more careful in their choice of words. I don't think whatever is going on there in Washington is jinks. What I think it is, if it's anything at all, is hanky-panky. Don't look it up."

"Why not?"

"Because," she said, "I have a pretty clear idea of what hanky-panky means, and I don't want you and the dictionary spoiling it for me."

LOCAL GIRL LAUGHS AT SUB-URB HARDSHIPS . . .

When Noonah Nummi Klx left her home on South L'vum street two years ago, she knew that adventure lay ahead of her as a Peace Corps worker in the remotest areas of the United States of America.

At her home last night she told of some of her experiences, while exhibiting specimens of native crafts which had delighted this dark-eyed, outgoing twenty-two-year-old charmer.

"I was assigned to what is called in America a sub-urb. It is hard to explain exactly what it is unless you understand that years ago these sub-urbs were settled by a group called the P.T. and A., with a subordinate but closely related sociological constellation known as the Little League," she said.

She then went on to explain that many of her efforts were directed toward changing the age-old, deeply-ingrained patterns of living.

"The father in the sub-urbs," she said, "leads a very degraded life. He must cook in the back yard on primitive equipment, often merely a basket or bowl containing charcoal. He is forced by the matriarchy to wear garments symbolic of his subjugation. These most often consist of a white apron embroidered with magic incantations. Sometimes his hands are restricted by large, padded gloves, as a further mockery of his natural role as a man who can hit out at forces which threaten the home.

"He then carries the food indoors to his wife and children and their friends. He serves them and they make insulting remarks about his cooking. I have talked to some of these husband-servants and they say they are not really hurt, that this is the way it has always been, even in their fathers' times. Urging them to rebel was, I discovered, useless, since they are so accustomed to degradation.

"While the women and children eat at elegantly appointed tables, the men squat in the darkness outside, gnawing their food and drinking a rather tasteless and mild native brew directly from tin cans. I noticed that when the women drink this 'beer' it is served to them in glasses, but the men sip directly from the can. When I asked them if this was their highest aspiration they merely shrugged and rolled their eyes."

Indeed, Miss Klx brought back with her a set of 12 "beer cans," interestingly crafted, each with two triangular holes in the top through which her guests inserted straws and enjoyed a delicious yak-milk frappé. Her parents, Mr. and Mrs. El Nafad Lx, have decorated their living room with original "bumper stickers" that their career-oriented daughter brought back from her sojourn in the wilds.

"Really," said pretty Miss Klx, shrugging her shoulders, "I gave up in my effort to teach them elementary hygiene. I remember one family where the child had a badly spotted face. It looked to me like pungy-yarba, but in their language they called it 'measles.'

"I told them I would take a calabashful of pig marrow and put it on an anthill. They would have nothing to do with it and called for what they call a 'doctor,' an amusingly solemn young man with a black satchel and a contraption he put in his ears. I had to sneak out that night and put the calabash on the anthill. A few days later, the child, naturally, was quite all right. I stifled my laughter when they gave all the credit to the 'doctor' and even sent him a sum of money."

Some of Miss Klx's stories seem hardly possible in the twentieth century. She told of rites where the men were forced to go out and sleep on the ground with groups of young boys called 'Cubes' and eat cold sausage and pretend to like it. She assured her listeners that she was not exaggerating.

All who meet her are impressed with this young lady's dedication. Although she is enjoying the comforts of her parents' hut and the company of old friends, she is eager to get another assignment in the United States.

"There is so much that needs to be done in the sub-urbs," she sighed, "and so little time to do it."

ENOUGH TO MAKE A MAN FLUSH WITH RAGE . . .

"They have done it now," cried Sam Irate, a local thinker, as he pounded the morning paper and the breakfast table with his fist. "I could see it coming. I could have issued warnings, but nobody asked."

"Who has done what?" his wife inquired.

"The professors, that's who," her husband roared. "The overeducated, tax-supported nincompoops of the intellectual establishment.

"They are attacking, by Aunt Nora, the American home. First we have these teach-ins hacking away at our foreign policy, then they have this sex research practically destroying the family, now it is the home itself, the very heart of the American Way of Life."

With a trembling forefinger he pointed to a headline: "Research Team Criticizes Design of U.S. Bathrooms."

"Well, dear," his wife said mildly, "sometimes I think—"

"Think, woman? Think?" he yelled. "You don't think about something like this. You believe, you feel, in your heart you *know*."

And he thumped himself on the cigars as he sought for words.

"I am firing off a rocket to our Congressman to see if any of my hard-earned tax dollars went to this so-called Cornell University, an obvious hotbed or anyway crypto-hotbed of who knows what all."

"Maybe," his wife ventured, "bathrooms aren't perfect. I sometimes think—"

"No," her husband snapped. "That is negative thinking. Once we start to doubt the American bathroom, what is left of the basic assumptions upon which we operate? We have a proud heritage in our bathrooms, and never mind the giggles, you there, young wise-apple. You are typical of your generation. Send a boy or girl from a fine decent American home away to college and they come back filled with a lot of fuzzy-brained pseudo-thinking by professors who if they don't like the plumbing here why don't they go over to Russia?"

"It doesn't say anything about Russian bathrooms, dear," said his wife. "It's just that these men at Cornell have some suggestions for improving—"

"Improving," her husband snorted. "Next it will be improve the Grand Canyon and the Rocky Mountains and the Statue of Liberty and Disneyland. That's what your improvers will do once they get started. As for Russia, sure they don't mention Russian plumbing, they're too smart for that; you have to read between the lines.

"Remember when we took that trip around the world? I'll bet you won't soon forget the way I handled a lot of those foreigners we ran into. Like in France it was champagne, in Australia it was kangaroos, in Japan it was kimonos. When I'd had about all of it I could stand, I shut them up in a hurry by reminding them that plumbingwise America reigns supreme."

"Some of the Japanese bathrooms . . ." his wife began.

"Adequate," Sam Irate said. "But for that matter they can run you up an adequate kimono in Brooklyn. No, sir, the minute we start criticizing the American bathroom we are a long way down the road of destroying the American home, and when that's gone, what's left?"

"The American garage?" his son asked.

"Very funny. A very intellectual-type college-boy wisecrack. Now they're criticizing the bathroom. Next it will be the living room, the kitchen, the pantry, the basement, the bedrooms, the front hall. Everything—all gone."

That was when the water started dripping on the breakfast table. Sam Irate glared at the ceiling.

"Is that shower pipe leaking again?" he wanted to know. "You'd think somebody could figure out a shower pipe that doesn't leak. I'll fire off a rocket to that plumbing company they'll never forget."

"Now, dear, calm down," said his wife.

"Yeah, Dad," said his son. "You're sounding un-American."

Sam Irate glowered, finished his coffee and put the empty cup under the dripping water.

A WORD TO ARCHITECTS, MAN-TO-MAN . . .

People who design houses are always asking typical women for advice, and typical women are always saying that they want a window over the sink so they can see what the birds, flowers and other neighbors are up to. Nobody ever asks typical men for their suggestions, which might open a few eyes.

A typical man might well say:

"The window over the sink is a punk idea for several reasons. In the first place, I married the girl for her to wash the dishes and make the lasagne, not to be goggling out the windows at some bird or other.

"Having a wife who watches birds is economic ruin. You

come home after a hard day at the wherever and she rushes to meet you with some rigmarole about having spotted this bird with a blue head and speckled wings. She has been looking it up in Audubon and whom-all and telephoning around about it, and as a result, not a dish got washed nor a can opened, and you have to eat out that night at some place where the cheapest entree is $1.19.

"Another thing, a man comes home and, as he is putting the car away, his attention may be diverted by a disc jockey on the radio telling him that the situation in Viet Nam is fraught with interest and he whangs the fender a little bit on the side of the garage door.

"Well, normally, he could let his wife take the car the next day and later could say, 'For heaven's sake, Mildred, look at the big gouge you have gouged in the fender.' But if she has this spyhole over the sink, she is at him tooth and nail the minute he walks in, accusing him of whanging the fender on account of having had a telltale beverage or two for lunch.

"Another point, which we might as well face, is that there are men in this country who occasionally wash a dish. They are not ashamed of it, unfortunately, but they would prefer to have an impenetrable brick wall between them and the public gaze while they are doing it.

"The window over the sink means that they are performing to a rapt audience of children, meter readers, passing strangers, smart-aleck neighbors, dogs, cats, squirrels and birds.

"Show me a house with a window over the sink, and I will show you a house where the architect didn't consult the mister."

✳ It's no trick to distinguish between antiques and old junk. An antique is something that has been handed down in a wife's family; old junk comes from the husband's side.

THE STRUGGLE TO LAG BEHIND THE JONESES . . .

A problem that a man must face occasionally is that his neighbors are all fixing up their houses and he must decide what to do about his own without (a) doing any work or (b) spending any money.

The trick, or maybe that's not the word, the procedure is to give the impression of a great deal of constructive activity, while avoiding (a) or (b).

I have a few suggestions. One is, if you see somebody painting a house on your block, you telephone down and say, "Sam, what is the name of the people who are painting your house?"

He tells you, and you ask, "What is their telephone number?"

He says for you to wait a minute while he goes out and checks, and you pretend to write it down. Then you say, "I like the job he's doing. He's working with a pink there that not everybody could get away with."

You haven't actually said, or even hinted, that you are going to paint, but the word quickly gets around that you intend to, and that in itself may get you through the summer. If the neighbors start getting restive you can call up, along in July sometime, and say, "Uh, Sam, I seem to have lost the slip where I wrote down the name of that little painter who did such a tremendous job with the difficult pink on your house, would you mind letting me have it again?"

If he runs any kind of a typical household, he has lost the number by then and you can say, "Well, Sam, I don't blame you. You got a terrific painter like that, naturally you want to keep him to yourself."

You have him sort of on the defensive there, and next time

your wife sees him, she can say, "We've been looking around for a painter. It's too bad people aren't more helpful."

Again, this starts all sorts of wildfire rumors that you are about to refurbish the mansion.

If he does have the number, you write it down and thank him. Either way, you may be able to postpone things until the bad weather sets in.

Another good thing to do is to walk around your house, choosing a time when you get maximum exposure to the gaze of the neighborhood. Look up at your house, kick the downspouts, flake off a little paint with a thumbnail. This is extremely persuasive, because why would a man walk around and look at his own house unless he was intending to do something to it?

It is even better if you can have a friend or relative unknown to the neighbors come over and bring a carpenter's rule and a pad of paper. He can walk around with you and the two of you can poke at things and measure them and he can write them down on the paper.

Talk that you are letting down the tone of the block will pretty well subside if people see businesslike activity of this type going on.

It is often helpful to put a wheelbarrow in front of the house, along with maybe a few old paint cans, a tarpaulin and a ladder. Who then can doubt that great plans are afoot?

Or you can import friends from outside the neighborhood to walk in and out of the front door, giving the impression that you are spending vast sums of money on the interior of your home. This may persuade the neighbors to excuse the shabbiness of the exterior.

A useful idea is to put a couple of "Fresh Paint" signs on the house, or to lay some two-by-fours on the front steps to give the impression that they have been newly concreted.

Ask your wife to call up people and say, "We'd love to have you over, but we're just so torn up."

She hasn't exactly said that you're having the place improved, but the implication is there.

Other ideas will occur to you. They should be inexpensive and enable you to put off any actual work until the neighbors finally come around with a rope.

OF COURSE, SENATOR VEST NEVER KNEW PANCHO . . .

A man who doesn't have a pet feels somewhat out of the conversational swim when other people are talking about theirs.

Like somebody will say, "Why, Poochy, my weimaraner, is almost human. He will bark when he wants to go for a walk and go get his leash and then he stands by the door."

It is nice to say, as I now do, "That is very cute and I know what you mean because my Pancho does the same thing."

"Is Pancho," they will say, "a Chihuahua or one of those other bright little breeds from south of the Border? A Mexican hairless, for example?"

"He is indeed hairless," I say, "and probably Mexican, although I prefer merely to say that he is of Latin extraction."

"And he barks to be let out?"

"No," I say, "he clicks."

"A clicking dog?" they inquire. "I do not believe I have encountered the species."

"Pancho is not a dog," I reply with frigid dignity. "He is a bean, although I try not to say so when he is in listening range. He thinks he is human, just like everybody's cocker spaniel. Sometimes, to get a laugh, I call him a human bean."

"You have a pet bean?" they inquire.

"Yes," I say, "but not, of course, an ordinary bean. Pancho is a jumping bean."

At this point a clicking is heard, and I take from my pocket a little plastic box containing four jumping beans.

"Which one is Pancho?" an observer will ask.

"What do you care?" is the natural rejoinder.

As a matter of fact, I am not sure which bean is Pancho, but he is the leader of the pack, if that is what jumping beans come in. All I know is that if you want a neat, clean, unobtrusive pet, the jumping bean is the man for you.

In the short time that we have had Pancho and his friends I can say that there have been no complaints from the neighbors about their flower gardens being trampled. It has not been necessary to put newspapers on the floor, to buy expensive pet foods, invest in rabies shots or city licenses, or send them to obedience school.

When we take a vacation, the jumping beans don't have to be boarded at the vet's. They can be taken along in the pocket.

Only when I am traveling by air do I leave Pancho at home. This is because clicking noises upset airline stewardesses and anything that upsets airline stewardesses interests the FBI.

On these occasions, my wife says that it is a great comfort to her to have Pancho in the house. He is a wonderful watchbean. Should an intruder enter the premises, he emits loud, warning clicks. At least I assume he would. I can't be sure, because the situation has never arisen. But you can't be completely sure even with a large and ferocious dog, can you?

We have all known people who had animals they claimed were watchdogs and all they ever barked at was the mailman or the water-meter reader and when a burglar came along they licked his hand. Pancho hasn't yet been tested, but I have every confidence in him.

I don't pick up Morse code too easily, but I am convinced that Pancho clicks out messages. Why should you laugh? Other people say they are getting messages from their doggie or their kitty cat or their myna bird.

How do I know that in my bean, the larva of the *Carpocapsa saltitans* moth, there does not dwell the transmogrified soul of an old telegrapher?

I don't like to be sentimental, but when I am discouraged, blue, sitting by myself in my study, Pancho clicks comforting clicks. Others will tell you how their dog puts his cold nose in their hand at such a moment, or their cat purrs, or their canary chirps.

Well, to each his own. In my case I get the same reassurance from Pancho's compassionate and empathic clicking.

Pancho doesn't care that I am not rich or famous. He does not take, he gives. Should fortune flee and friends prove false, and all the other pets in the house turn on him, the man with a jumping bean always has a buddy.

I would never let Pancho down. I try, perhaps in vain, to be a better man in order to justify his trust.

And when the talk turns to pets, I am proud to tell about Pancho, my jumping bean. It puts a pretty sudden end to that phase of the conversation.

MY DAUGHTER'S HAND? I'LL GIVE YOU MY FOOT . . .

I grew up in a happy era when girls' fathers took only one attitude toward the boys who called on their daughters: They were all bums.

It was a little wearing at times, but at least it was consistent. We knew where we stood.

The father of a lovely teenager tells me that it is all different now, and he admits it must be difficult for the young men who drop by his house.

"It's the fault of all this reading we fathers have to do to keep up with the subject," he explained. "When you and I were young, the fathers of girls didn't have to check the newspapers, the magazines and the latest books to find out what we were like. But now a father of girls spends most his time in research on boys.

"Take my daughter's friend, Eric. Two weeks ago we had a speaker at the Kiwotary club who said that today's young men were the finest in our history—intelligent, decent, hard-working, ambitious. He urged us not to be influenced by the small minority who go around slugging elderly storekeepers with tire chains. Give credit instead, he advised, to the 99 per cent who do not even own tire chains. He said we should encourage today's youngsters instead of all the time knocking them.

"When Eric came by for Eloise Jane that Friday night I offered him a cigar, told him how proud I was of him and the rest of the space generation and said if he ever needed $5,000 to buy a telescope so he could open his own astronomical firm I would go on his note. Eric seemed pleased, though somewhat dazed.

"The next time he showed up he came in like he was some sort of a cross between Albert Schweitzer and Rock Hudson.

" 'Just a minute, Daddy-o,' I said, 'roll up your sleeve.' He said, 'What?' I said, 'I want to see if you been mainlining. I know all about you boys from the better suburbs.' He said, 'You call this a better suburb?' Well, I told him to straighten himself out or never come back again.

"I'd been reading what low, vicious, cunning animals these young men are today. Drugs and who knows what all. In fact, we'd had a speaker at the Optilions club that week who showed the various firearms that these people who come around calling on our various innocent daughters habitually carry on their persons.

"Naturally, Eric was alarmed. The next time he showed up he was afraid to come in. He just honked his horn outside the house. I rushed out and said, 'You low creep. Haven't you any more respect for a girl than to honk a horn for her? If you haven't the common courtesy and politeness to call for her properly, well, then, all I can say is, it's certainly a reflection on your common courtesy and politeness.'

"The following Saturday he came to the door, neatly dressed, hair combed, polite as can be. 'May I please ask for the privilege of having your daughter, Miss Eloise Jane's hand for a malt and movie, sir, Your Majesty?' he said, like butter wouldn't melt in his mouth.

"He might have got away with it, too, except that I had read, meanwhile, how the polite boys are the very worst. Can't trust them a minute. So I made Eloise Jane and him sit right there and watch the teevee all night where I could keep an eye on them."

I asked this man how things were at the moment between Eric and him.

"I'm taking him bowling tonight," he said.

"What have you read about American boys to lead you to this decision?" I asked.

"Nothing about American boys, but I read a long, authoritative article about American girls," he said, "and I'm taking the poor kid bowling to protect him from Eloise Jane."

✷ Trying to describe his daughter's new boy friend, an acquaintance says he looks like a sketch by a police artist.

✷ The current trend in fashionable weddings is toward the type in which the bridegroom says the bride's father seems like a nice young man.

LET'S GO SLUMMING AT YOUR FOLKS' HOUSE TONIGHT . . .

Some authoritative lady was saying the other day that the modern young couple was doing more formal entertaining, with the meals in several courses and pickle dishes on the table and big plates under the little plates. She interpreted this as a return to a more gracious way of life, perhaps aided by the many easily prepared dishes now available in the grocery-store's ice bin.

I don't think this is it at all. It's because the modern bride is given so much cutlery, chinaware and crystal that she has to use it. The thing is that the couple moves into a small apartment, or even house, and the shelf space is limited. But there are enough glasses, tureens, oyster forks and fondue skewers to stock a jewelry store in a medium-sized metropolis.

There is room in the cabinets for only about half the stuff, so the rest of it has to be kept dirty all the time. The only space for it is stacked on the drainboard.

It seems to me that every time I go to a wedding the happy couple is being launched upon a sea of alcoholism. There are two dozen glasses for everything from cocktails to liquers, by way of champagne, beer and toddy.

Every possible viand that could decently show up on a civilized menu will be speared, shoveled or slit with the appropriate silver utensil.

The bride flunked brownies in Home Ec, but she has a complete set of apothecary jars loaded with basil, sweet marjoram and other spices. Only two months ago the bridegroom attained the estate where he could purchase a six-pack of beer legally. Now he rejoices in a set of ships' decanters, each with a dog tag around its neck, engraved with the name of an expensive booze.

They may be budgeted down to the last tube of toothpaste, but there is a wine chiller that will hold a jeroboam, and a dish designed exclusively for caviar.

All of this is fine, to be sure, but it offers an interesting reversal of the generations.

The young couple goes over to the home of one or the other set of parents. There the elderberry cordial comes in cheese glasses and the food is served on a set of earthenware from Dish Night at the Gem Theater in 1938. For their wedding the parents got four plates of their chosen pattern and one complete place setting of silver. Over the years they have added enough so that they can now serve coffee to four and iced tea to three. Making out a guest list is a challenge. If there are to be eight at table, there has to be at least one on a low cholesterol diet, because there are only seven butter spreaders.

At the old folks' is where the living is informal. What with bracing up the children's teeth and endowing their education, there never has been time to complete the full set of cut-glass compotes that Aunt Ella started with a resounding one.

At this stage of their lives, when they can at last perhaps afford it, there seems to be little point in stocking up on such trivia as a sterling silver socket for the ketchup bottle or a peppermill so tall it has to be brought in through the window.

In their young married years, the parents had to go to their own folks' houses to get a glimpse of snowy linen and table settings where some of the silver was on one side of the plate and the rest on the other.

They themselves kept house with crockery and jelly glasses. Now, for a touch of the true graciousness, they go visit their children in whose homes everything is a four-color dream out of *Lovely Living* magazine.

"Our generation," a man of middle years remarked the

other evening as he salted his macaroni from a saltcellar marked Souvenir of Excelsior Springs, "has been bracketed between eras of elegance. Pass the paper napkins."

MELTED DOWN, A WIFE IS WORTH ABOUT $1.89 . . .

People who think up these recurring statistics about how much a wife is worth if she had to be paid wages strike me as selling the darling considerably short. They will put down, for example, baby-sitting at 50 cents an hour, secretarial duties at $1.25 per same and laundry at $10 a day, or whatever figures they may choose. It usually adds up to the fact that the little creature is worth about $150 a week, just for duties such as these, to say nothing of the sunshine of her smile, which we'll leave out of it.

This is shockingly short of a wife's true worth. A good wife is a lawyer. She goes to the man who sold you the Whambang and she will say, "Charlie, you unloaded a terrible car on us which makes funny noises when it starts which it seldom does and I am either going to sue or scream quite a bit and maybe throw myself down on the floor of your luxurious showroom and kick my heels."

Charlie says, "Lady, we'll fix the car."

Now this is much better than a mere husband could do. He would go in and say, "Uh, Charlie, do you suppose there might at the slightest outside hangnail of a possibility be any chance that there is something wrong with this zingy think-young model you sold me?"

Charlie says, "No."

The husband says, "I thought not."

From then on the family is stuck with the lemon of the car. Or, if he should go out and get a real lawyer, all it would be is an exchange of communications and a legal fee on top of all the other expenses.

So on deals like this, I figure the wife is worth a $25,000 retainer as a lawyer. In this capacity she also gets mangled shirts refurbished by the laundry and the insurance company straightened out on why it should put a new roof on the house.

Wives just naturally do these things better than husbands. Make it $30,000 a year.

Also they are doctors. A husband will come home feeling no particular symptoms except he is a little weary, and he will get a quick prescription:

"What you need is a few fast hands of canasta with Claude and Clara Callous. It will be a grand tonic for the system. We can have dinner on the way over to their house at a medium-priced eatery."

And he often survives.

Or he may feel worse than that. He may have a sore throat and a touch of fever and spooky feelings in his extremities. The wife says, "Poor dear, you must curl up immediately in bed with an aspirin, but first bring in a few armloads of firewood and do something to keep the second-floor shutter from banging. I'll hold the ladder. Plenty of rest is the important thing."

After a few days the fellow feels better.

What do doctors make a year? Let's stick to averages. After all, this isn't a society practice. Put it down for fifteen big bills.

In addition to being a healer, the wife is a psychiatrist. A man says, "I want to go bowling tomorrow night." His wife says, "You're nuts." If there is only one session like that a week, it's still $50 each, or about $2,500 a year.

Don't marriage counselors make good money? They couldn't get by for less than $25,000 a year. Wives are the greatest marriage counselors in the world. A husband will say, "There's something wrong with our marriage." She answers, "It's your fault." What's left to be said?

I mean, this business of saying wives are worth some ridiculously small amount a year because they chauffeur the kids and so on is, well, ridiculous. They are not only lawyers, doctors, psychiatrists and marriage counselors but also other highly paid professions. They are tax advisers. True, their main advice is, "Don't pay it," but at least it's advice. They are engineers. They tell you how you can carry the six-foot-wide bureau through the three-foot door. These are not piddling occupations.

The way I figure it, the average wife is worth, easy, $185,-000 a year.

****

REPORTS FROM THE
CULINARY FRONT

Or: Who smuggled the cuisine into the mess hall?

****

When people call me a gourmet they smile, which is all right. It's only when they laugh out loud that it hurts. A measure of my eating style is that I like my steaks well done. This preference infuriates chefs, as is widely known, and often brings them out of the kitchen brandishing a cleaver—particularly in the East, where a thin veneer of civilization covers a tribe of ravening devourers of raw meat.

In the Middle West we grow up in close affinity with the beef creatures. When you have known someone well you don't care to eat them until they have been decently incinerated. The Middle Westerner's standard response to the uncooked steaks preferred in more sophisticated milieus is: "I've seen cows hurt worse than this live."

Why anyone should pay $4.50 to be served a cinder is beyond the understanding of the possessors of more refined palates. The explanation that I don't intend to taste anything but the ketchup anyway only makes the culinary purist recoil further.

Another offense of the Middle Westerner is drinking his coffee with his meal instead of waiting until later. We also do something odd about the salad, such as eating it before the meal or not, I forget which.

However, regional dietary peculiarities seem to be fading, along with differences in speech and dress. I needn't tell you about the progress in transportation and food-handling techniques, which brings seafood to the Middle Western table where it once was a rarity. This development is hailed as a great advance by those who like lobster, oysters, clams and such matters.

My own view is that if it had been any part of the divine plan for us to eat those things the Lord wouldn't have hidden them away in the vasty deep, where I am perfectly content for them to remain.

But, here again, a lot of ketchup helps.

As people move more freely around the country we are broadening our gustatory spectrum. One of the lasting accomplishments of the Truman administration was the popularizing of bourbon in the East. It became, for a while, a snob (or reverse-snob) drink in circles where scotch had previously held the franchise. "Bourbon and branch water" had never been a particularly usual expression in the bourbon belt, but it caught on as a bit of esoteric folksiness on the hitherto effete Eastern seaboard.

As a footnote to this subject, it might be mentioned that St. Louis and Kansas City are still the only major metropolitan centers where, if you want soda in your drink, you had better specify seltzer or you will get lemon pop. I am always delighted by wealthy Texans and Oklahomans who carefully specify their scotch by brand name and then ask to have it mixed with Coca-Cola.

In recent years New York has made some tentative moves in the direction of topless waitresses, apparently on the theory that it was O.K. because it was an importation from San Francisco, an In city. Thirty years and more ago in Kansas City, the Chesterfield and Winnie Winkle clubs featured businessman's blue-plate luncheons served by waitresses who not only were topless but bottomless as well. Several severe cases of optical indigestion were reported.

These prefatory remarks are intended merely to establish the shaky foundation that underlies the following handful of comments on the restaurants and dining-out customs of America.

TURN UP THE JUKEBOX AND TURN OFF THE
ATMOSPHERE . . .

A friend who offered the other evening to take his wife out to dinner left the choice of where they would go up to her. With only one provision.

"I won't go any place," he said, "where they have decor."

"You don't have to order it," she said.

"I'm not talking about something on the menu. I'm talking about the decor. The *mise-en-scène,* as I see it is called in the fancier spots. I don't want to eat in any place that wafts me."

"That whats you?"

"That wafts me into another century with its tradition of fine eating, or into another land with its tradition of gourmet service," he said. "I want to go to a restaurant where the waitresses are dressed like waitresses not like page boys from Camelot or sexy squirrels."

"I guess," his wife said, "this lets out the Crossbow Inn, where everything is carried around on a flaming halberd."

"I guess it does," he said. "But any place else."

"Well," she said, "I've been wanting to go to the Glockenspiel Bierstube."

"There's got to be an umlaut in that name somewhere," he said, "and I'm allergic to umlauts. Anyway, I'm pretty sure that they put lederhosen instead of paper pants on the lamb chops. Anywhere else will be O.K. It's your night out."

She mused her way through the ads and tried to remember the names of restaurants her friends had recommended.

"How about the Robinson Crusoe Room?" she asked. "It's all gotten up so cute, like a regular desert island. The menu is written in the sand and in order to attract the waitress's attention you have to take off your shirt and wave it.

"Please," he said. "Any place at all, as long as it's not cute. Surely there must be somewhere left where they just want to give you food."

"The Cowpoke Corral?"

"The chandeliers are made out of wagon wheels," he said. "I haven't been there, but I know that they are, and the bar stools are covered with pinto horsehair. On the men's-room door it says Wranglers and on the other one is whatever is the feminine of wranglers. Look, this is a large and cosmopolitan community. There surely must be some place where we can get away from decor."

They had some trouble, I can tell you. They uncovered a place called the Bivouac where everything was served in surplus GI messkits. One spot offered nothing but Gambian food, and, since the economy of Gambia is founded upon the peanut, the only thing on the menu was peanuts. This fellow's wife called to verify the fact, and the people were very nice. They had a take-out department and would rush as many peanuts as necessary to their front door right away.

"Don't misunderstand me," my friend told his wife. "I love the gay adventuresomeness of extoic cuisine. After this mood passes I suppose I will go back willingly to places where you sit on cotton bales instead of chairs or where the menu is written with charcoal on the back of a shovel. But just for tonight —no decor."

There were a couple of near misses. His wife phoned a place called Sam's which sounded promising, but it turned out that they had Chinese lanterns.

Finally, in desperation and hunger, they left their house and drove around. Finally they spotted a diner. Just a diner. No decor.

They went in and sat down.

"Nice place you have here," my friend said to the counterman.

"Glad you like it," the counterman replied. "This place used to be just another Chinese Colonial tearoom with Aztec overtones. But we've redone the entire decor."

"The what?" my friend gasped.

"The decor," the counterman said. "We had a decorator from New York do it. It's now a completely authentic early-American diner from the 1920s."

✳ Power failures remind us that dining by candlelight is romantic only when there's a choice.

WHEN HAUTE CUISINE GETS REALLY HAUTE . . .

No building, whether it is a high-rise apartment building, an office structure, a hotel or even a hospital, has any status unless the whole massive pile culminates in an eating place. The noontime traffic in the elevators once was mainly people going down to lunch. Now they are going up to the Cloud Room or the Sky Lounge.

The most common name for these culinary palaces in mid-air is the Top of the Something-or-Other. If nobody is feeling particularly original, it is the Top of the Address. Like the Top of 320 or the Top of 11864 East.

The main feature of the decor is glass. You sit there at a table next to a glass wall and look out across the street and into the restuarant on top of the building opposite.

You say to the waiter, "That sort of livid-colored gunk the gentleman over there is eating looks delicious; what is it?"

The waiter says he doesn't know but he'll telephone across the street and ask. Your wife may complain that the Top of 893 looks taller than the Top of 890, where you are.

"The people over there are looking down on us," she sniffs. Where she used to complain that you never could get a good table, she now whines that you can't even pick a top floor.

You're just as glad the people across the way are higher, because looking down gives you vertigo. There's no use in asking for a table away from the window, especially if you are with people who are showing you the place as a treat.

They ask what is the purpose of going to a restaurant on top of a building if you don't look out the window. And that's certainly a reasonable point.

But it makes it pretty tough on a man with acrophobia, eating the entire meal with his eyes closed.

✳ The corner cafe, which changes its name with the fashions, has gone from Atomic Eats to Orbit Lunch to Psychedelicatessen.

WAIT UNTIL I SLIP INTO SOMETHING POLITE . . .

They have been doing some research out at Las Vegas into the public relations of the staff at the casinoes and bars, and the answer is that the fewer clothes the waitresses are wearing the less polite they are.

I think any of us reasonable people could have told them that. How polite can you be when you are freezing to death, which is possible even in Las Vegas, what with the air conditioning and all?

The report goes on to say that "scantily clad waitresses are more civil to women who act cheaply than they are toward women who appear well-bred and proper."

Again, I think it figures. A well-bred, proper woman is going to say, "Why, dearie, you'll catch your death, half nekkid like that. Here, let me throw my tippet about your poor old shoulders."

The cocktail waitress is naturally going to resent this sort of thing, as it takes a lot out of a girl to run away from Plum Nellie, Ga., in the first place, without having somebody who looks like her Aunt Sue making a fuss over her.

Not that nudity and rudeness necessarily go together. The armed forces have long recognized that the best way to make a man polite is to take his clothes away from him.

The army early caught on to the fact that an unclad man is going to be very courteous and say "Yes, sir" or "No, sir," or whatever the answer may be, on the theory that the less trouble he causes the sooner he is going to get back into his trousers.

Doctors operate (oh, we have to be very careful of double meanings here, don't we?) on the same principle. That's why the first thing they say to you is "Undress." They know that the patient bereft of clothing is going to be docile.

A man who can be overbearing in a two-hundred-dollar suit is going to be a lamb when all he is wearing is the pelt that was issued to him free at birth.

All of this is perhaps aside from the point of the Las Vegas findings that the more clothes a waitress wears the politer she becomes. Or maybe it isn't. Possibly the scantiness of the garb isn't the point at all.

In fact, I have just decided that it isn't.

You take a nice girl, polite and all the rest, and you dress her up in a dress that reaches from her neck to her toes and you put a lei around her neck and a Russian fur hat on her head and tell her she is now a waitress at a place called Old Mother Hubbard's Hawaiian Samovar, and you are going to have a discourteous employee on your payroll.

Waitresses, like anybody else, don't want to look silly. A girl walking around with about half enough clothes on in a roomful of fully dressed people looks silly. And a drunk shouting "Voom! Voom!" doesn't help any.

But she would feel just as silly if she were wearing any other kind of strange get-up.

You go into a store where they are having a special Lincoln's Birthday sale and all the clerks are wearing stovepipe hats, and you will find a surly bunch of clerks.

Visit the bank when everybody is wearing a button that says "Friendliness Day," and you had better not ask for a loan.

Waitresses have it the worst, because so many of the places where they work feature a decorative motif that requires them to dress up like Martha Washington or a Roman slave-girl or a Gay Nineties soubrette or a flapper from the '20s. Small wonder if this makes them rude.

In other words, I feel it's the quality of the clothing, not the quantity. A waitress wants to dress like a waitress, just as a lawyer wants to dress like a lawyer or a carpenter like a carpenter.

What ruins the politeness is not the nudity but the nuttiness.

WHEN IN DOUBT, EAT WHERE THE STRANGERS DO . . .

A vacation tip: If you know anybody in the town you are visiting, don't call them until the very end of your stay when you need a free meal or, at worst, a check cashed.

Otherwise, what happens is this: You call old Joe and Mary Lucretia. Gee, it's tough, they would love to see you but this is their bowling night. This fact doesn't bother you, particularly. They have every right to bowl. Nobody can expect them just to sit by the telephone waiting to hear from visitors out of the long ago.

But what they could do is hang up. Instead, they feel this

inner guilt-ridden (why guilt-ridden? What's wrong with bowling? They need to bowl don't they? They have to stay in good shape and live a long time for the sake of the children. They should be proud to be bowlers, but they have this little annoying sensation that they are not being hospitable enough, whence the guilt) need to guide you in their city.

"Where are you going to eat tonight?" Mary Lucretia inquires.

"Why," says your wife, "we thought we would eat at Luigi's, which we have just read about in this wonderful write-up it got in the *Holiday* magazine that was on the plane, and it got three stars or bells or whatever it is that *Holiday* gives restaurants. It said that the Shrimp Escritoire was the specialty and that Max, your maître d'hôtel, would recommend other delights and it was all candle-lighted and the ambiance was terrific. The moment we got in town we called the library to get a definition of ambiance, and it's O.K., Mary Lucretia, in case you write your mother about our being here."

Of course, Mary Lucretia, on her way to the bowling lanes, where everybody is going to have a Pecky-Cola and a hamburger, says, "Oh, my dear, you don't want to go to Luigi's. That's where the tourists go. Everybody knows that the moment a restaurant gets mentioned in a national magazine it's through."

Your wife puts her hand over the horn and tells you the situation.

"Does Mary Lucretia," you ask your wife, "mean that the minute they see the piece in *Holiday* the whole kitchen force starts cooking as bad as possible? Suppose nobody in the place subscribes to *Holiday?* We might luck out."

"Mary Lucretia," your wife says, "is merely trying to be helpful. After all, she and Joe live here."

"They've lived here six months," you point out. "Just since

Mammoth Chemicals transferred him. And, frankly, I feel that a man may be a Mammoth chemist and a fine bowler without necessarily being much of a gourmet."

"But," wails your wife, "they're local!"

"So," you say, "ask the local where the locals eat."

She does and jots down the address of the Shoo-Fly Café, a five-dollar cab ride from the hotel. (Luigi's is just across the street.)

The specialty of the Shoo-Fly is Salisbury steak, which they are out of, but the stuffed pepper is very nice.

The next day you meet another local who asks where you ate last night. Rather proudly you mention that you have avoided the run-of-the-mill, highly-publicized spots, and dined at the Shoo-Fly Café.

"That tourist deadfall?" he cries. "If you had only let me know, I would have steered you to Luigi's."

"I thought Luigi's was for tourists," you say.

"It used to be," he explains, "but it got so many tourists that it got a name as a place for tourists so that they all went to the Shoo-Fly Café and all us genuine built-in locals eat at Luigi's."

All of which is why I tell you to go into the town, eat where you want to and forget it, insofar as your digestion will permit you to.

I am a little conscious of this matter because of a recent few days in New Orleans, where I couldn't get any of the locals to agree on which of the world-famous French Quarter restaurants I should patronize.

Finally, the most local of the locals said, "Frankly I wouldn't eat in the world-famous French Quarter at all."

Which is when I decided to ignore all the advice and eat right in the heart of the French Quarter, a delicious hot dog and a chocolate milkshake.

****

A NONCOMBATANT IN
THE WORLD OF SPORTS

Or: Make touchdowns, not war

****

You'll have no trouble spotting me. I'm that easily recognizable type, the old athlete now run a little to fat. But still with that amazing grace and agility of movement, the balance, the lightning reactions, going to the left like a giant cat, juking the linebacker out of his shoes, showing a little hip and then taking it away, playing the big game with the booming serve, ice water in my veins, reaching back for a little extra, taking all the punches on my arms and elbows, reading the defenses, judging the fly by the crack of the bat, the mental stopwatch clicking, the pulse beating slower than the average man's.

Yes, well, I am sorry to have deceived you. Except the part about running to fat. It can happen to nonathletes, too.

Because the truth about it, and never mind what I used to tell my children before they were old enough to wise up, is that I never was much of an athlete.

I did win the intramural half-mile once and even had a medal, which is around somewhere. But I'm not like people who still are called Lefty or Moose on account of having been a pitcher or fullback. You will meet people who are known as the old hurdler or the ex-pole vaulter thirty years after the event. Nobody greets me with "Well, how's the old ex-intramural half-miler?"

I guess what I really am is a spectator (gone to fat). Spectators are what is wrong with America, we are told. Participants in various sporting events will often pretend that they are, somehow, better than the spectators and try to boss the spectators around by telling them what brand of deodorant to use.

My feeling is that if there weren't any spectators there wouldn't be any sports. Who is going to put a shot or knock somebody else down if nobody is watching?

Our country could get along without athletes, but we'd be in a sorry fix without spectators.

✳ My word to physical-fitness enthusiasts is that muscles come and go, but flab lasts.

✳ Texas has a rather confusing image. It's the country of rugged outdoors people, where they play baseball and football under a roof.

A RUN AND JUMP THROUGH HISTORY . . .

An Olympics year always stirs interest in the events of track and field, which, ordinarily, American sports fans relegate to somewhat subsidiary concern. I am glad to see these occasions roll around, because I feel that track is a sport that deserves a little more enthusiasm than it customarily receives.

The way I reconstruct it, somewhere in the old, old days, before the invention of the wheel or much of anything else, there must have occurred the first free hour, when our ancestors had nothing to do.

People write dissertations today about how leisure is misused. Just think how it must have been for man of the Dawn Age who had never had an afternoon off.

Let's say for the first time enough meat has been killed, enough firewood dragged in, and there's all this time hanging heavy. Here are a couple of Piltdowns or whatever, sitting around the door of the cave and asking themselves what in the world they are going to do.

So one of them says to the other, "Let's invent athletics."

The other says, "All right. What sort?"

The first one ponders a while and then says, "Well, we can get five guys on a side and they'll run around and bump into one another and fall down quite a bit and every few seconds another guy will blow a whistle and they'll all stop until he blows the whistle again."

"What's a whistle?" asks the other caveman.

It's sound history that basketball is a very ancient game. The Indians of Central America had the equipment—the ball and the hoop—but they didn't have a whistle. Basketball can't be said to have really established itself as a sport until the invention of the whistle. (The striped shirt was invented shortly before the whistle and may have had something to do with its development.)

Nor can I see football as the oldest of sports.

Surely one of these Cro-Magnon types isn't going to say, "I'll tell you what, Gursh, let's think up a sport so complicated that nobody can understand it, and we'll have two explainers to explain it to the people."

Gursh would then say, "Why would we want to do that?"

"Because it would sell a lot of beer."

Football, I'm afraid, was beyond the brutish imagination of our remote progenitors. It requires a sophisticated audience. It is the great spectator sport it is today because it addresses itself to a society that admires the nonobjective in art and the esoteric in poetry.

Football fans watch the game to be confused. In primitive

days, merely living was confusing enough; they didn't have to think up a game to compound the situation.

Nor can anyone seriously suggest that those cavemen would have started out with a game in which there are nine youths on a side and every few innings an old man walks out and takes the ball away from one of them and signals for a left-hander to come in.

I don't think they could have grasped the concept of baseball, except for the part about killing the ump. Which suggests that two of our most ancient sports probably are wrestling and bashing people with clubs. They still exist, but in radically different forms. Wrestling has moved over into the area of entertainment and bashing is illegal unless done under the proper local, national or international authority.

And this leaves track, because these two olden-timers might very easily have said to one another, "I can beat you running to that tree," or "I can throw that boulder farther than you," or "I can jump over a higher bush than you can."

So we have track, the oldest and purest of sports. The oldest for reasons I have just demonstrated. The purest because, unlike in other games, there is no necessity for a rules committee to reinvent it every year. Also there is hardly any professionalism. It is unlikely that the fastest hurdler or broadest jumper will ever make a dime out of it, which should be a consolation to all true sports fans, if not to the athlete's parents.

Oh, and incidentally it is a good thing all this running and jumping was invented before the wheel. If it had waited until after the invention of the wheel probably nobody would have ever bothered doing it in the first place.

✳ In every basketball season I sound a call for sanity. Allow each team 30 feet of player on the floor at any one time: Five 6-footers, or three 7-footers, a 5-footer and a 4-footer, or any other combination that computes.

HOW ARE YOU GOING TO BEAT MERCURY IN THE
SPRINTS? . . .

We may be able to get past the Olympics of 1968, but from
'72 on it's going to get chancier and chancier. I mean that our
horizons are expanding, and before long, just having athletes
from one planet, and a minor one at that, won't afford a truly
representative competition.

You may say that interplanetary participation will make
the games just that much more interesting, and you would
be right, but there will be problems, too.

Look at the way it is now. Every country that has a sport it
is particularly good at demands that it be a part of the Olympics schedule. Moreover, they understandably regard their
own specialty as the really Main Event.

In the United States we think it's all track and field or
swimming, with a few other events getting a nod if we happen
to be good in them that particular year.

Other nations couldn't care less about these events. With
them it's bicycle racing or canoeing or soccer. If they win in
any of these they consider that they have won the Olympics.

Well, what is going to happen when the great opening pa-
rade of the Olympiad includes the boys, girls, and things from
Mars, Venus, Jupiter, Mercury and the moon? People who
raise money for stadiums, field houses and halfbacks assure us
that sport is essential to life. If, therefore, there is life on these
planets, then there must be fun and games.

So, if the popular sport on Venus is throwing the Nblrx
through the Narf, would it be fair to expect their splendid
athletes to compete only in such events as the javelin or the
eight-man crew?

Some of these people from elsewhere may be only about a
couple of centimeters tall, and it's asking quite a bit of them

to participate in equestrian events, where they would have a tough time handling the horse even if they perched in its ear.

They're bound to be a game bunch, as are all Olympic athletes, and they might compete in high diving, which could be dangerous on a windy day when their little crowd-pleasers could get blown clear out of the aquatic arena.

Or I can imagine bad interplanetary relations arising when the moon sends down its ace high jumper who has been winning all the cups and gold medals back home with jumps of thirty feet. He goes to the Olympics here on the earth and he will run into our type of gravity and will clear only about five feet. The lunar sportswriters will send back bitter dispatches about unfair jumping conditions and knocking the arrangements in general.

Or would it be fair for a sprinter from Jupiter to be forced to keep all six of his feet behind the starting line when the earth athletes are only required to have two back there?

Beyond that, if the participants from Outer Space compete in what we regard as normal sports, the least we can be expected to do is challenge them in theirs, whether it is throwing the Nblrx through the Narf, the 1,000-meter Gronch or the game of Kransabi.

Most of our colleges don't have the 1,000-meter Gronch even in intramurals, and where can you find a Narf to throw a Nblrx through, even if you had a Nblrx? Since a Narf is, as I understand it, a hoop three miles in diameter, building one for the Games would certainly add to the expense, but if it's what they do best on Venus, throwing the Nblrx can't be left off the program.

I'm not bringing this matter up in order to frighten the Olympics committee but merely to suggest that it may not be too soon to start preparing for the inevitable.

A REAL ALL-STAR FAN . . .

One of the best things about me is that I may be the only fan who likes these football games between all-star aggregations or teams representing the North vs. the South, the East vs. the West, the Southeast against the Northwest, or whatever the geographical juxtaposition may be.

Most people say these are no-good games because there is no identity. The teams are a conglomeration of this person and that, and how are you going to fix your loyalties?

But I cherish these contests as dramas of how complete strangers can work together under stress. It warms my heart to see young men who have barely been introduced give their hardest tackles and flashiest runs in loyalty to an ephemeral cause. It is the spirit that welds disparate individuals together in an emergency, such as blizzard or power failure.

To do and/or die for the good old team is one thing. To do it for a bunch of casually assembled athletes guided by a strange, or even inimical, coach is another matter. There is something almost biblical in being able to say, "I was a stranger and you blocked for me."

So while others devote their most intense support to the college or professional corporation of their choice, I prefer to turn my attention to those occasions that pit random group against random group.

Modern writers tell us that ours is an alienated generation, which is why it makes sense to cheer for the Disaffiliated vs. the Unattached.

BRIDGING THE BRIDGE GAP . . .

I remember as a small boy looking up at the first star of the evening, saying the mumbo jumbo about star light, star bright and making the wish that never in my life would I have to play a game of bridge. And this is the only one of my boyhood wishes that has come true.

The point is mentioned because I want to make it clear that I have no deep personal involvement in the way the Italians keep humbling us at the bridge table. Just the other day Italy defeated us in a 60-deal final match by a score of 158 to 112. I have no idea what this means. In fact, I sort of had the idea that what won in bridge was the lowest score, getting caught with the fewest cards in your hand, as in rummy (unless I am wrong about rummy). But apparently the big score wins and this means the Italians have swept the World Bridge Olympiad.

I don't think there was bridge in the first Olympics, in fact I'm pretty sure there wasn't. In those days the athletes performed without any clothes on. I'm not putting that in to be racy. It's the truth. For that reason (no clothes) there was no giant slaloming or bridge playing. Great Scott, no bridge player would want to make it appear that he was playing strip poker, and unsuccessfully at that.

I have every respect for the opinions of nudists, but I think they will admit that the Olympics never really became much of a commercial success until the participants started wearing at least their underwear.

In the World Bridge Olympiad, I don't know what they wear. I imagine that the women wear large flowered hats (among other things) and the men have blazers with the insignia of their bridge frats embossed upon the handkerchief pocket.

It's not important what they wear. Except that most of the reports I get from bridge players go into details about the costuming, such as that Alice Lou wore the same frock at two meetings in a row.

But let's forget that part of it; what really hurts is that, according to the news item from which I am extracting all this, the Italians "have dominated international bridge for the last decade."

What are we doing about it?

Usually, here in this go-ahead country, when we see a gap we start to close it. When the Russians put the first Sputnik into outer space we erased everything from the curriculum except algebra and started begging the big airplane and electronics companies to take our tax dollars to get us up there higher and faster.

As soon as the British, Australians, etc., started running the mile in four minutes or less, we yanked everybody away from the algebra books and started them running. Now we are not only running the mile with alacrity but have enough athletes left over to catch up with the rest of the world, almost, in tennis.

But nobody (or nobody I am aware of, at any rate) is working toward a massive breakthrough in bridge. It's enough to infuriate a man, seeing our young people hanging around the public library or doing push-ups or building model rockets, when they should be playing bridge.

Italian children go right home from school, sit down at the table and say, "Ho Kay. Whosa deal?" (O.K. Whose deal?)

There are young men and women right here in this affluent society of ours who don't know a Vanderbilt convention from a grand slam. I don't either, but it doesn't matter, because I am too old. By the time the next World Bridge Olympiad comes around I would be dozing over the first chukker, or whatever a round of bridge is called.

Too many American mothers are setting a bad example for

their children by spending time in the afternoons in the kitchen instead of being out playing bridge in a patriotic manner. Fathers of America, how long has it been since you went and played a few hands of bridge with your son?

I'll bet the Russians aren't being apathetic about this matter. In the struggle for the minds of men it is going to do a nation very little good if it leads the world in automatic washing machines but goes down doubled and redoubled (a technical term, I am informed) at the bridge table.

Let's get to shuffling before it is too late.

TOUGH YARDAGE IN THE VAST WASTELAND . . .

One of the great values of the Monday-morning newspapers is that they sort out for you what it was you saw while watching the weekend sporting events on television with another two or three going on the radio.

And now a new element of confusion has been added.

Let's say it is a third down, short-yardage situation. A tense moment, as you well know.

What a man hears at this point is: "A murder aboard his yacht brings suspicion on Millionaire Playboy Mickey Rooney and presents a challenge to Defense Attorney Walter Brennan in tonight's episode of 'Perjury,' the continuing story of our rotten legal system and now Quarterback Schnark goes for the bomb in an effort to gain field position."

A voice of a married lady in the kitchen calls: "What happened?"

About all a man can reply is, "There was a murder on Mickey Rooney's yacht and Schnark went for the bomb."

"I don't mind you gluing yourself to the tube all day," says the married lady's voice, "but you'd better lay off the sauce."

The wear and tear on the family fabric may easily be imagined.

Or one sportscaster will say, "Well, Al, the Monsters stayed on the ground in the first quarter but failed to move the ball. Do you think that in the next period they will make greater use of the rifle arm of their all-conference quarterback Shotgun Simpson?"

His partner replies, "Yes, Norm, it will be interesting to see about that. A pretty but domineering movie star is admitted to Big Town Hospital and refuses to submit to an operation which Dr. Rip Torn considers necessary to save her life. Debbie Reynolds guest stars Wednesday night in another exciting episode of 'Malpractice' on this network."

"Thank you, Al, and now the kick-off is a booming end-over-ender."

"That sounds great," says the voice from the kitchen.

"Yes," says the man, "it puts the Crawdads back deep in their own territory."

"No," says the voice, "I mean about the pretty but domineering movie star and her operation."

It doesn't happen only in football, of course. On baseball telecasts you hear:

"Manager Maelstrom is coming out of the dugout and he is talking to his big left-hander, Hook Huckleberry, who seems to be tiring. A mysterious stranger appears in the barber shop of Fess Parker and as wild rumors about the robbery of the Virginia City Bank circulate through the community, preventing a lynching becomes a full-time job for the fastest shears in the West. That's on 'Frontier Barber' every Thursday night over most of these stations."

In these changing times when issues, crises, pressures, tensions and the clash of rival ideologies are battering the minds of Western man, we are mixed up enough. So is it any wonder that a man arrives at Monday morning with all these, plus a mental jumble of end runs, T-formations, blocked punts and, in season, triples and stolen bases? Are we really helping him when we add yachtboard murders, domineering movie queens and lynch mobs?

"HEY, GARÇON, THIS HAIR OIL IS SLIGHTLY CORKED . . ."

Everybody at the table is naturally accustomed to Delahanty opening his remarks with what is wrong with the country. Usually it is something creeping, such as creeping socialism, creeping automation or creeping bankruptcy due to his wife buying a new lampshade.

"Delahanty," Cromwell Boggs has told him on occasion, "your dear mother must have been frightened by a caterpillar before you were born. Anything that creeps gets a low mark in your books."

"I don't like creeps either," Rose, the waitress, customarily puts in, giving meaningful glances while the assembled gourmets are trying to make up their mind whether they want a hamburger with cheese or a cheeseburger, hold the cheese.

"Well," said Phil Plimmer on this recent noon hour, "what's creeping today?"

"The noodle soup," said Delahanty.

"Not really?" asked Cromwell Boggs, apprehensively.

"I'm ordering the soup," said Delahanty. "What's creeping is champagne into our most cherished and one hundred per cent American activity. I refer to baseball."

"Yeah," said Phil Plimmer, "I'll take the tuna supreme, Rose. I been reading about how whenever a ball team wins something on the order of a pennant or a series, corks are popping all over the dressing room like it was Maxim's."

"I believe," said Cromwell Boggs, "there is the late golfer known as Champagne Tony."

"I'd believe anything about golf," said Delahanty. "It has a champagne-type country-club background to it. There is nothing creeping about champagne in golf or tennis or, of course, bicycle racing, which is a very big sport in La Belle. But somehow it doesn't seem to fit in with what I like to refer to as the National Pastime."

"It's true," said Phil Plimmer, "that the game's anthem mentions no beverage except soda pop, although I often notice beer mentioned in connection with it on the radio and television."

"Maybe some champagne company could take over part of the sponsorship," said Cromwell Boggs, "and on the commercials we could see the nifty-quickhanded shortstop taking a sip of the bubbly and telling how he likes this brand because it tickles his nose."

"I think they've got a code," said Phil Plimmer, "which says the boys can't indulge commercially. All they can do on camera is shave or comb their hair."

"The way I picture it," said Cromwell Boggs, after pausing to order a grilled cheese sandwich, medium well, "is that a couple of the boys would be having their regular after game comb-out, and the old slugger would inquire of the neophyte, 'Still using that greasy kid stuff?' And the kid would say, 'No, I'm using Chateau LaFoof, '53,' and he would haul up a magnum and pour it over the veteran's head. The big thing to remember is that, if you give the stories of these clubroom celebrations a close reading, you find out that the athletes use the champagne to pour over one another more than they do as a beverage."

"That's easy to say," said Delahanty darkly, "but these things creep. They start using champagne for hair oil and next thing you know they're drinking it."

"Drinking hair oil is an older American tradition than baseball," said Phil Plimmer.

"One thing," said Rose, picking up the dimes, "there's no creeping inflation at this table."

✶ A sportswriter says that rookies in the professional football training camps are often lonesome. And 285 pounds of homesickness is a lot.

✳✳✳✳

UP FRONT WITH
THE POLITICIANS

Or: Government, world affairs and other fun topics

✳✳✳✳

Calvin Coolidge's famous pronouncement that the business of America is business has long since been outmoded. The business, as well as the national sport, of America is politics. Everyone carries a political chip on his shoulder, and under each chip is a political bug.

The government was once a remote entity with activities that were largely irrelevant when they weren't hilarious. In the last thirty years it has become increasingly personal. It has moved into our homes, our mailboxes, our pockets, our pay envelopes and our schools. It is constantly on the alert to protect us from the perils of Poverty, Peace and Privacy.

Politicians and reporters don't really get on very well together, no matter how many swimming pools they may push one another into. The reporter knows that when the going gets difficult the politician will cry that he has been misquoted, and he probably was, as reporters are kindhearted creatures who know that about the most ruinous thing you could do to a politician would be to write down exactly what he said.

My line of work, then, has made me suspicious of all politicians. This attitude, of course, does not cause the soul to blossom nor the hard, gemlike flame of zealotry to burn. On the other hand, it saves a lot of disappointments.

Watching government in operation is almost enough to turn a man into an anarchist. The only trouble is that I have never figured out who, in an anarchy, would collect the trash, fix the streets or protect the meek from the rapacious.

Of course, these things don't always get done in our democracy, but at least we have some telephone numbers we can call. If the only satisfaction we get is being transferred to another number, we still have the feeling that we are doing something. Telephoning a branch of the Government at any level is pure McLuhanism; like a stone through an embassy window, the medium is the message.

The man who takes his stance as an observer of politics cannot help but admire those who follow causes with single-minded devotion.

I am reminded of the lady who wrote to inform me, with suitable scriptural citations, that the end of the world was set for the following Tuesday. She also adorned her letter with stickers demanding the immediate repeal of the income tax.

Under the circumstances, I could only stand in awe of her dedication.

⁂ Congressman Sludgepump calls his spacious home Context, so he can always claim he was quoted out of it.

DON'T JUST EXERCISE YOUR FRANCHISE, TAKE IT FOR A ROMP IN THE PARK . . .

We all realize that the big crumb stuck in the throat of democracy is that not enough people get out to vote, and I think it is time to do something constructive about it instead of just passing resolutions and putting up billboards.

Look at one angle. We have drive-in movies, drive-in laundries, drive-in banks, drive-in almost everything. Our society recognizes the value of the drive-in principle in everything except voting. And voting is, after all, the Name of the Game. It is why this country exists.

Yet there are no drive-in places to vote. Why not use, let's say, the drive-in eating places and let those nice carhops come out and receive your ballot? The judges could be inside next to the guy who yells "Two cheeseburgers on No. 3," and they could validate the vote. I wouldn't close the drive-ins down. Let the voter have a tomatoburger while he exercises his franchise. Why should it be a sacrifice?

We lock the tavern doors on Election Day, but is this wise? By and large, these are the most comfortable premises a community affords. Cut off the drinks, if you prefer to think people would vote sillier when drunk than they do sober, but at least let the citizens enjoy soft lights, a jukebox or maybe a strolling violinist and upholstered chairs while they vote.

In precincts where there are no commercial establishments we could still liven things up some. If the voting is being conducted in somebody's garage we could have a little jazz combo of local youngsters or, if nothing else, the homeowner's child could play the piano.

We have been so afraid that the vote would be corrupted that we have made the polls antiseptic to the point of dullness. Outside of a certain inner glow, there is nothing you get out of voting, especially if you are the kind who consistently votes for losers.

Vote buying is frowned upon and yet vote buying fills a vacuum. The more upright political leaders have failed to make voting fun, so the venal bosses step in and at least make it profitable.

Our voting system is so obsessed with democracy that it

makes no provision for snob appeal. If you want to buy a pair of slacks on a sale, you get a note from the Busy Bee Department Store saying that as an old and valued charge customer you can come in a day ahead and have first pick at the racks before the door is opened to the general public and people who pay cash.

Think of how it would feed the ego to get a note along these lines:

"We here at the election commission have been thinking of folks like you who have voted with us for many years, and to show our appreciation we are inviting you to drop by and cast your ballot on Monday afternoon. This Special Voting Privilege is not transferable. It entitles you to vote at your leisure without the tiresome waiting to which the general public may be subjected on Tuesday.

"Refreshments."

Nothing, it seems to me, would make a man more eager to participate in the great democratic function of voting than something like this, with its implication that he is getting in on something not available to everyone else.

Voting by mail has been suggested, but I'm not too sure about it. People tend to lose stuff that comes in the mail, and there's no glamor about it.

Why not spend a little money and have girls to greet every male voter with some such remark as, "I am your Vote Bunny. Let me show you how to operate the machine"? For the ladies there could be Tony Curtis types to perform the same service.

Appeals to duty, to good citizenship, to the memory of 1776 don't seem to get folks out. We apply the techniques of Madison Avenue to the primaries, to the conventions, to the campaign; why not put them to work, as well, to bringing people into the polls?

WHO PULLED THE PLUG ON THE SEA OF INTELLIGENT
FACES? . . .

A sad scene, oft captured in the press photograph, on the
giant eye, in the novel and on the stage, pictures the after-
math of the election. The defeated candidate, shorn of emol-
uments if an incumbent, frustrated in his hope for perquisites
if an aspirant to office, sits alone among the wracks and tatters
of his dreams.

After the long campaign in which his hand has been
clasped by those who voted for his Daddy or whose Daddies
voted for him, in which he has been referred to by others than
himself as the nation's hope, when his opinions have been eagerly sought by solemn teen and cold-eyed ward boss, when
his every step has been dogged by the alert newshawk, he de-
scends to the reality of the bare hall with its bedraggled posters, its overdue rent, its cigarette butts, its crumpled coffee
cartons.

Visions of glory have departed; not only the captains and
the kings have fled, but the Assistant Chairman of the
Mothers-for-Sam Sausage; the snappily dressed Sausagettes,
and the Regional Coordinator of the Opposition Defectors
for Sausage. All, all are gone.

It must be difficult for a man who has seen his name on a
thousand shopping bags and his face on a thousand bumpers
to realize that this name and this face, instead of belonging
to the nation, are now back as his own personal and slightly
shopworn property.

But if it is a hardship for the candidate, think awhile of
the plight of the voter. This heartbreak, this deflation, hit the
candidate only if he loses.

The voter feels the letdown no matter which side wins.
And he goes through it at every election. Only the most per-

sistent of losing candidates is likely to experience it more than a handful of times.

We are told that it is a cold awakening for the candidate, who has been surrounded by sycophants and flatterers constantly magnifying his ego. And it may be, but the butter is spread even thicker over the voters.

Before the election, just a few brief days ago, who was the voter?

Why, he was the man who had built the country, who had sailed its seas and plowed its prairies, raised its bridges, toted its barges, won its wars and forged its steel.

Everything, he was told, depended on him. If, in a simulation of modesty, he were to say that his vote amounted to nothing, he was informed that his vote was the greatest vote that had ever swayed an election. On him, he was told, depended the freedom of the world, the preservation of the peace, the defeat of communism and a multipurpose dam across Hog Wallow Creek.

If the candidate was inflated by his own publicity, how about the voter, who had been told throughout the campaign that he was a thinking man? If he were only given the facts, according to the candidates and their speech writers, he would instantly know what to do about everything from Cuba to pesticides, from medical bills to wheat surpluses.

The candidate, after all, often gets intimations that he is not universally regarded as infallible. He will read rude things that his opponent has said about him. The fact, indeed, that he has an opponent demonstrates that he is not unanimously loved.

But no one, during the campaign, hints that the voter is anything but perfect in all things—well informed, patriotic, selfless, hard-working and dedicated. His face is described as intelligent, his children saluted as kissable and his wife alluded to as a lovely lady.

Then comes the election, and what is he? Just a cipher or—

less than that—a taxpayer. That's why we are always sorry to see an election campaign end. One day we are lauded as that noblest flower of civilization, an American voter; the next we are at best an ungrateful constituent, and more likely a selfish vested interest or a pressure group.

And, unlike the candidate, we do not even have any balloons with our names on them to take home to the children.

AND AN INSTANT REPLAY OF CAMPAIGN PROMISES?

Richard M. Nixon has said that if he had his life to live over again he would be a sportscaster. The concept of the statesman-sportscaster is an intriguing one, and if we continue to improve modern man, maybe we will produce a satisfactory combination of the two disciplines.

In that event, we might have this sort of State of the Union message:

"Good morning, budget fans. Well, sir, it looks like another great year here in the nation's capital. In the weeks ahead we are going to bring you such outstanding features as an open-housing bill, a surtax and an all-out war on poverty.

"What's that, Mel? It sounds like a whale of a schedule? Indeed it does, Mel, and let me also say what a whale of a privilege it is having you alongside me as majority leader in bringing all these fine features to the folks out there.

"Just as a little background, folks, I think you'll find it interesting that this is the largest Federal budget ever tossed into the hopper by a left-handed President on a Wednesday. I think that's right; just a minute while I check the record book. Yes, that's right, folks, so you see we are making history here today.

"And may I say parenthetically that this is a beautiful day for history making. It's a little cloudy, of course. In fact, it was raining when we came into the Capitol today, and there is a crosswind of about fourteen miles an hour. But I was talking to a member of the Cabinet a few minutes ago and he told me he didn't expect the weather to be a factor.

"Well, that's the way it looks from the White House, folks, (Am I still on, Ed? O.K. Wind it up?) but before I sign off I want to say congradulations to everybody connected with this fine presentation here today and to thank my spotters from the House and Senate. Now, over to you, Mr. Speaker, in Legislative Control."

✳ Easter is a particularly busy time at the White House, with the children rolling eggs on the lawn and the police picking up nuts at the gate.

NIPPING NEPOTISM IN THE BUDDY . . .

Among many reasons for handing it to the ancient Chinese, in addition to their invention of paper and fireworks, is that they thought up a wonderful addition to the concept of civil service.

The Chinese had competitive examinations for government jobs as far back as the fourth century B.C., and good for them. But the point is that there was a little rider sort of snuck into the legislation. Anybody who sponsored an applicant who couldn't pass the test was punished. It is in this addendum that I hear a kindred spirit hollering down the rain barrel of history.

It strikes me as the answer to nepotism and political finagling of all kinds. The Big Cigar who foists his nephew or his wealthy friend's nephew upon the civil service board ought to suffer if his candidate turns out to have been wasting everybody's time.

Let the sponsor of totally unequipped job applicants live in dread of the telephone call:

"Your honor, your sister's youngest boy has just scored the lowest grade ever registered in the memory of veteran observers. A committee will be around tomorrow to duck you seventeen times in the village pond."

Next time he may be a little more selective about whom he recommends.

DROP THE BRICK, NOT THE BOMB . . .

Some umbrage has been taken because a British magazine in the toggery trade has criticized President Johnson's suits. Slurs of this kind are, of course, regularly exchanged. Certain boors, for example, spoke unkindly of Princess Margaret's wardrobe when she visited us, and a late lady columnist once was disdainful as regards Mrs. Khrushchev's mode of dress.

Cries of bad taste often arise when incidents of this kind occur. Do we criticize the dress of our friends? As a matter of fact, we do. Setting that aside, however, the consensus is that a little more charity in knocking the choice in clothing of foreign dignitaries would be a good idea.

I disagree.

What I would suggest is a cabinet-level Secretary of Minor Insult, with counterparts in other governments. We do not permit civilians to drop bombs on foreign friends or sink their ships. This is in the hands of elected officials. And this is the way it should be with the Minor Insult.

The dream that possesses me is that we should develop the Minor Insult on an international scale to the point where it will take the place of missiles, guns, napalm and poison gas.

We may envision the scene in the Ready Room at the Minor Insult Department. The hot line rings. It is a spokesman for some oil-rich sheikdom. "Ah ha!" says the spokesman. "Infidel dog. Your President has wide lapels." Click!

Immediately the duty officer is buzzed. He hastens down, struggling into his tunic, and dials back the oil-rich sheikdom.

"Ah ha!" he announces. "The government of the United States announces that your sheik's mother wears army shoes." Click!

It may be that one big hang-up in international relations is that we have all this syrupy diplomacy going on, with everybody being polite, and when nothing comes of it the only recourse is to cry havoc and let loose the dogs of war.

It is a bad plan.

In our own lives, with whom do we get along the best? Obviously it is the man whom we address as "You old horse (or hoss) thief" and call other disrespectful names. The crime news should have taught us to beware of the politest boy on the block. He is the one who is saving up shotgun shells for his near and dear.

Fat Jack Leonard, just as a suggestion, comes to mind as the first Secretary of Minor Insults. Someone of that caliber, certainly, should be in charge.

When greeting the French head of state, the Secretary would say, "Pardon me, monsieur, is that your nose, or are you eating a banana?"

To the visitor from the Far East in his native robes: "I know the invitation was 'Come as you are' but this is ridiculous."

I offer these only as examples. Men skilled in the art of insult will do much better. The goal is as obvious as it is humane. Men and nations who are swapping insults about trivialities—dress, table manners, grammar and so on—are far too involved to deliver the Ultimate Bomb.

Consider this angle: If a man insults your neckties or your wife's figure, you aren't going to annihilate him nuclearly because of it. There's always the chance that you would think of the proper snappy comeback after it was too late.

Peace through Minor Insults may be a program that will work.

LATCHING ON TO THE POT IN INTERNATIONAL POKER . . .

Disarmament conferences would be a lot livelier if our negotiator had a little Tlingit blood in him and the Russian representative was perhaps a Kwakiutl, if only on his mother's side.

The way things are going now each side tries to hold onto every little old airplane or missile it happens to have, and about the only thing specific is a proposal that we will toss 480 B-47s into a bonfire if the Russians will burn up a similar number of TU-16s, both of which I take to be airplanes that don't have much of a future anyway.

Chinchiness of this type would run counter to the traditional belief of the Tlingits and Kwakiutls, as well as of the Tsimshians, Nutkas, Bella Coolas, Yuroks and other tribes, which we may lump together as the North Pacific Coast Indians.

Chiefs of these tribes would invite other chiefs to potlatches, tremendous feasts at which they would show their wealth by destroying stuff which was highly prized but which they didn't really need, such as copper plates, furs, blankets, rattles, masks and so on.

The more wealth a chief could destroy the higher his status rose. If one of them got up and destroyed six copper plates the other chief would say, in effect, "Shucks, look at me destroy eight copper plates."

To what grand heights might not our international confrontations rise if, instead of suspicion and niggardliness, they operated on the basis of the potlatch.

Imagine our representative getting up and saying "O.K., there, Igor, or whatever your name may be. We got two B-70s and we're setting fire to both of them."

The Russian, somewhat shaken, will have to say, "Two measly B-70s? We are scrubbing our entire moon project. How you like that, short sport?"

Our boy, coldly contemptuous, will reply, "Big deal. As of six o'clock tonight we are pulling out the plug on all our Polaris-class submarines."

Think of the status that would accrue to the country which first announced that it was scrapping five hundred ICBMs and twenty-three anti-missile missile installations. It would drive the other countries crazy.

In potlatching, the giving of extravagant gifts is as important as destroying symbols of wealth. If a chief offers a magnificent present, the one for whom it is intended cannot refuse it, and must bestow an even more elegant token in return.

Let's picture the Russian saying, "You in the West worry about Hungary; so take it," and we answer, "Thank you very much. Vietnam seems to have caught your fancy. It's yours."

It will be a wild scene. We'll give them the Baltimore Orioles; they'll counter with Valery Brumel and the Dynamo soccer team.

We'll blow up Hoover dam and they'll blow up the big one on the Dnieper. We will score incalculable status points by publicly immolating five million automobiles, seventy-five thousand refrigerators and a billion bathtubs, leaving them nothing to counter with.

Driven to desperation they will cry, "All right. We're tearing down the Kremlin tomorrow."

With the curled lip of contemptuous disdain, our man will say, "Stuff like that doesn't impress us. We've set fire to Disneyland."

SIGN THE POVERTY BILL WITH A CHEAP PEN? . . .

To get maximum impact from the legislation Congress is churning out, the President is contemplating signing major bills in locations other than Washington. The pattern was pretty well set by the signing of the Medicare bill in Independence, Missouri, as a tribute to Harry Truman. Exciting vistas open before us.

When Congress passes a water-pollution bill, it would seem to be a natural for big-time news coverage, with TV camera crews, the slick magazines and so on to the saturation point.

Lady Bird has already had some experience with scuba diving, and there seems to be no reason why she couldn't accompany her husband on a subsurface signing occasion. Whether Hubert Humphrey is sinkable is a question that we may leave undecided for the moment. Leaders of both houses and both parties will be there with oxygen tanks strapped to their backs. Everett Dirksen will send up pear-shaped bubbles. If the Secret Service should have any reservations about holding the ceremony underwater, it might be done on water skis, as the entire entourage skims over a polluted lake.

Agricultural bills will be signed on the farm, educational measures in the schoolroom and transportation legislation standing up on a bus.

It's hard to see any objection to the idea, outside of the cost, which is a question that only comes up among curmudgeons who fail to appreciate the fact that the President and his traveling troupe have to be somewhere, and it might as well be out among the real people as in Washington.

HOW ABOUT CHOOSING ONE IDEA FROM COLUMN NO. 1
AND ONE FROM COLUMN NO. 2?

Since this is the age of the kit and the package deal, it is no enormous surprise that the concept applies to ideas as much as to automobile accessories or toilet articles.

The two hottest items are the Right Wing Kit (A) and the Left Wing Kit (B). They contain certain standard opinions.

Kit A is as follows: Escalate the war in Vietnam; stop fluoridating the water; impeach Earl Warren; throw the beatniks out of the colleges; repeal the income tax.

Kit B provides the client with these concepts: Get out of Vietnam; civil rights for all; folk singing; fluoridate the water; beards as a sign of campus involvement.

I'll admit I have never discovered the logic that binds these ideas together. But it is a handy shortcut in social relationships when you can tell whether or not a person is likely to be for or against water fluoridation on the basis of preferring Lawrence Welk to Joan Baez.

The visitor from abroad is impressed when you are able to predict that the man he has just met and who recommends dropping a nuclear bomb on Hanoi also wants Earl Warren impeached.

"What does Earl Warren have to do with Hanoi?" the visitor will ask.

"Nothing really," you reply, "But it comes in the package."

The same visitor might think it rather eerie the way you base a pretty good guess as to a man's views on the voting laws of Alabama on the fact that he has a guitar in his house.

About all you can do is confess cheerfully to the stranger from overseas that none of this makes any particular sense except as a demonstration of prepackaged thinking.

There are signs, however, that there may be a growing revolt against the Idea Kit.

A friend of mine was telling me the other day of his experiments in this direction.

"What started me thinking about it," he said, "was when I looked in the pantry and saw about a hundred little packages of Chunkie-Wunkie breakfast food. I foolishly asked my wife, 'Who eats all the Chunkie-Wunkies?'

"She replied, 'Obviously nobody.'

"It turned out she had been buying the assortment, which includes little packs of Snicky-Snackies, Chicky-Chips, Crispy-Crunchies, Oatsie-Toasties, Flicky-Flakies and Chunkie-Wunkies.

"There was at least one member of the family who liked one or more of Snicky-Snackies, Chicky-Chips, Crispy-Crunchies, Oatsie-Toasties and Flicky-Flakies. Nobody liked Chunkie-Wunkies, but we went on buying them because they were part of the package.

"I got to thinking that I had been buying the handy intellectual six-pack, and that I was getting several ideas I didn't want along with those I did.

"For example, I am in favor of strong action on civil rights, but I am also for a strong policy in Vietnam. I don't want fluorides in the water but I don't want to impeach Earl Warren either. I think college students should be committed to something more challenging than panty raids, but I abhor folk singing."

"You mean," I said, "you're going to take the opinions you want and reject the ones you don't, even if it means breaking up the set?"

"That's right," he replied, "and we're buying our breakfast food the same way."

"Well," I said, "don't come by the house tonight. We're got a visitor from overseas and I don't want to get him confused."

SHADES FOR THE SHADES OF HISTORY . . .

One reason young people today have so little regard for our national heroes, such as Washington and Lincoln, is that they are shown in the textbooks without dark glasses. It is difficult for the kids to feel any kinship with them. A little retouching of famous portraits of the men who built America wouldn't hurt. Just the addition of wraparound shades would do a world of good in making these great figures seem close to the modern student.

Look at the pioneers, heading West the way they did, right into the blinding sun. Nobody under forty can understand why they weren't wearing dark glasses.

And politicians. For a while they were jittery about dark glasses on the theory that it made them look as though they were about to take the Fifth Amendment, but those days are long gone.

Let a candidate appear invariably in purple glasses, each lens as big as a TV tube, and he would sweep the election.

People who wear dark glasses are the majority in America today. It is time they had a chance to vote for One of Their Own.

THE HALF-FULL BOX OF CEREAL IS IDEAL IF THE KIDS
HATE THE STUFF . . .

I was congratulating a typical housewife of my acquaintance on the good news that the Government was going to protect her from being duped and flimflammed by dishonest packaging.

"No more," I said, "will you bring home the box of soap

chips and discover to your surprise it is only half full. Under proposed legislation the manufacturer will have to put on the box 'This Box Is Only Half Full.' "

"The poor thing," she said.

"Who?" I asked. "The consumer?"

"No," she said, "the manufacturer. Mr. Glug, or whatever his name is, that makes Glug, my favorite soap chip."

"You like it because of its sudsing action."

"Who cares about that?" she said. "Soap is soap, right? I buy Glug because of Mr. Glug, if that's his name. The poor guy only fills the box half full. The way I figure it, that's all the soap chips he can afford. Gee, I think about him a lot. I kind of picture how it must be when he goes home at the end of the day.

"His wife is standing there at the front window of their modest home and she can see old Glug coming down the block from the bus stop, and he's walking kind of bent over and dejected. Women can tell. She knows it's been another day when there were only enough soap chips to half fill the boxes.

"Of course, she feels this little thrill of pride in Her Man's integrity. What he could have done would be to have filled half the boxes, which would have meant the other half wouldn't have had any soap chips in them at all. And that wouldn't have been fair.

"Naturally, being the fine man he is, as Mr. Glug gets closer to the house he straightens up and starts whistling as though he hadn't a care in the world, and his kiddies rush out and jump in his arms and when he comes in his wife looks at him with lovelight in her eyes and says, so as not to alarm the little ones, 'How did it go with the b–o–x–e–s?' And he says, 'Not so g–o–o–d.' She gives him a pat of encouragement and they sit down to a meal at which the merriment is feigned.

"You think I could let down a man like that by buying another brand, especially now that he's going to have to stamp that half-full business on every box and let the whole world know about it? It was his brother-in-law's fault anyway."

"What brother-in-law?"

"Glug's brother-in-law. He's the one that bought all those big boxes without giving any thought to how many soap chips it would take to fill them."

"So," I said, "stick to Glug. But you are also going to be protected against packages where the picture on the outside is prettier than what's on the inside."

"They better not start messing around with my pictures," she retorted hotly. "Look right here. See this can of huckleberry popovers? It's got the greatest picture of huckleberry popovers on the label I ever saw. Every time I swing open the pantry door it does my heart good to see that picture of huckleberry popovers. It gives me a lift along the way, and goodness knows we need all the help we can get in these sorry times.

"Now I happen to know that the huckleberry popovers inside that can aren't nearly as handsome as the picture. So what does the Government want to do? It wants the poor soul who makes those huckleberry popovers to put a picture of a punk popover on the can. Would a punk picture on the outside make the popovers on the inside any better? I don't see how. All it would do would be to give me a punk popover picture to look at instead of a pretty popover picture. Is this what they mean by protecting the consumer?"

"They just don't want you to be misled."

"Is that the way it's pronounced?" she asked. "I always thought it was mizzled. Anyway, I guess the people in Washington mean well. I'll tell you what; I'll go along with their program if they'll get themselves straightened out first."

"In what way?"

"Well," the typical housewife said, "there are a lot of small politicians in big packages and a lot of political plans that don't fit the pretty pictures on the covers."

WHAT GOOD IS IT IF YOU CAN'T BREAK IT OR THROW IT AWAY?

Leading economic thinkers agree that the trend in this country, what with more people being born and machines doing more and more of the work, is toward a society in which there will be productive employment opportunities for only a comparatively small percentage of the population.

The emphasis, in a few decades, will have to shift from production to consumption.

Whereas the traditional American accolades have gone to the man who turned out the goods, we will have to start finding suitable rewards for the man or woman who buys them. Instead of cries of "More production" in shop and factory, the rallying slogan will be "More consumption."

Today's obituary notices emphasize the things a man contributed to the Gross National Product, the houses he built, the mousetrap he invented, the automobiles he assembled.

Fifty years from now we will have items such as this:

"Alfred Affluent, prominent local consumer, died yesterday at one of his three homes. Last year he was saluted by the Chamber of Commerce for his many years of dedicated purchasing.

"A friend, pointing to Mr. Affluent's 65 suits, 87 pairs of shoes, 4 automobiles, 8 television sets, 9 refrigerators and 26 air-conditioning units, said, 'We have lost one of the great ones. Al was never too busy to consume something else. It is consumers like Alfred Affluent who built this community.'

"Mr. Affluent was known as the consumer's consumer. Colleagues who quit consuming when the stores closed at five-thirty o'clock recall that he often diligently sought out places of business which stayed open later. As he was always waiting when shopping hours began in the morning it was not at all unusual for him to put in a twelve-hour day of solid consuming. Even on his lunch hour he managed to consume three lunches and countless martinis. He will be missed."

As indeed he will, because while a machine can produce, a machine cannot consume, except for a certain amount of electronic tape and a can or two of oil.

At the moment there are very few pure producers or consumers. There may be an eccentric producer or two who lives on nothing but peanut-butter sandwiches and wears discarded clothing, and an occasional playboy who produces nothing but headlines and fees for the divorce lawyers. But most of us combine some aspects of each.

In the world toward which we seem to be heading, however, the role of the average citizen will have to be that of the consumer only. It has already been predicted that by the year 2000 young people will go directly from college to retirement.

So we had better start training our children, at home and in the schools, to meet the challenge of the Age of Consumption. When the little boy spends too much money and comes back for a refill on his allowance we must pat him encouragingly on the head and say, "Only twelve years old and already he is throwing money around like a real pro."

Don't chide the child for breaking his toys, but praise him for his contribution to Gross National Consumption. Some day he will grow up and have the opportunity to break automobiles and major appliances. Because if people don't learn early the proper habits of buying things they don't need, breaking things that must be replaced and wasting all the bountiful products of our ever more efficient factories, we are going to be in a mess.

Where the nonproductive consumer of tomorrow is going to get the money to do all this with is a matter of minor concern which I see I do not have time enough to go into at this session.

WAITER, THE FBI PUT A BUG IN MY SOUP . . .

I am as ready as anybody to go along with the idea that there is entirely too much snooping and eavesdropping going on, but I must admit I can't quite see how this thing works of having the olive in the martini rigged up as a little microphone. A Senate committee heard about it the other day. There were other devices exhibited, but it was the martini that caught the imagination of the Senators and the press.

This may be because Washington is a martini town. There was no talk of rigging up the maraschino cherry in the Manhattan—the reason, obviously, being that the Manhattan is not an In drink in top-secret circles. Nor was the cherry in the old-fashioned suggested as a possible transmitter. One reason may be that the cherry in an old-fashioned doesn't have a toothpick in it, and I assume that the toothpick is a functional part of the olive-transmitter. It is the aerial.

And this is one thing that worries me. If you are saturated with Government information and are handed a martini in which the toothpick is about eighteen inches long, wouldn't you suspect that you were being broadcast, and not only locally at that?

Over the years, and as a matter of research, I have observed a world of martini drinkers, and I have never yet seen one talk into the olive. I have known them to mumble into their cuffs, into the bartender's ear and almost anywhere else, but never into the olive.

Besides which, about the first thing they do is eat the olive.

The very nature of the martini is that if you don't eat the olive before you drink the drink, you are going to get a toothpick in your eyeball.

So the victim of all this electronic scheming swallows the olive, with its transistorized broadcasting mechanism. What is the spy going to do? He can't very well yell, "Hey, you swallowed the transmitter. You got any idea what those things cost? You think olives grow on trees?"

At the other end, Igor, who is monitoring the tap, gets nothing but a lot of gurgling, splashing and undescribable echoes from inside the victim's stomach.

Also, how does the spy get the victim to order a martini? He may be a fellow who never indulges. Or he is on a diet and all he wants for lunch is a can of some kind of low-calorie liquid. Can the spy sell him on the idea of putting an olive in his dietary delight? It seems unlikely. Or suppose, instead of a martini, he orders a Gibson, which means that instead of an olive there is a pickled onion. Imagine the consternation among the comrades at the bar:

"Take the transmitter out of the olive and put it in the pickled onion, Nikita."

"Sorry," Nikita says, "we got direct orders. No substitutions. The transmitter stays in the olive until I get a release from Smersh."

Besides, I'm not sure you can put a microphone inside a pickled onion.

Aha! I see it now. It's not the victim's martini that has the microphone in it. The spy has this fake olive that he brings along and puts in his own martini. Fine. Except how does he get the victim to lean across the table and talk into a strange olive?

And isn't the victim going to wonder why the spy is waving the olive under his nose and saying "Louder. Speak right into the pimiento"?

No, I'm sorry. I just don't see how it could work.

Plus another overriding consideration. In all my years of observing martini drinkers I have never heard one utter a single line that any government, foreign or domestic, would pay a nickel for.

****

WARNING! YOU ARE NOW ENTERING THE EDUCATIONAL ZONE

Or: The future belongs to those who will be around then

****

All the years of schooling culminate for the young American in the commencement address. Here is where it comes to a focus. In about forty-five minutes, the distinguished orator gives the class the distilled wisdom of the ages and launches them upon the sea of life.

If the graduates will listen closely, this is what they will learn:

1. Although the world faces many problems, these are exciting times to be alive. The reason these are exciting times is because of these very problems. The speaker personally wishes he were as young as these fine young Americans because then he, too, could participate in the excitement and, well, yes, challenge of the years ahead.

2. We read too much about the draft-card burners and the marijuana users and the flaunters of dirty words and LSD. Well, the speaker believes, this is what sells newspapers. As a matter of fact, he wishes that people who write these things could be here today and look across this broad sea of intelligent, clean-out American faces. Then these people would real-

ize that the beatniks and the Vietniks are only a small minority.

3. The world outside these ivied halls is different than the world inside these ivied halls. Out there the world has no patience with the man or woman who settles for a mere "passing" grade. It is very competitive out there, the speaker feels.

4. The speaker is amused by recalling that when he graduated he thought he knew all the answers. This, he discovered, was not true. To be frank, the students are only beginning the process of education. That is why this ceremony is called a com-mence-ment. They may think that they are educated now, but the man or woman who ceases to expand his horizons, to think creatively, to exercise his brain will soon fall behind in the race of life.

5. When he was young the speaker was very poor. He did not have the many advantages which an affluent society has bestowed upon the class assembled here today. He knows the view is unpopular, but it is his personal opinion that it was those early hardships which molded his character and carried him to the pinnacle of success upon which he now stands. The pioneers, whom he deeply admires, were quite a bit like him in that respect.

6. It is the speaker's impression that the old-fashionable virtues of honesty, decency and regular bathing are now considered "square." If so, then he is proud to be square, because he has personally observed that his own lifelong devotion to honesty, decency and regular bathing has paid off.

7. Liberty is not the same as license, rights involve responsibilities and free speech does not entitle a man to holler "Fire," in a crowded theater.

8. Man's scientific progress is moving ahead in leaps and bounds. Major breakthroughs are at hand. And yet, the sober truth is that man's social and ethical progress is failing to keep up. The speaker agrees with all other thinking men that this is a bad thing.

9. While the speaker is not so vain as to believe that the members of the class will remember everything he has said here today, he does not feel the day will have been wasted if some remark of his will be of assistance to you young Americans as you go through life. They are, after all, things that he himself learned in work and study over more years than he cares to think about.

10. A sense of humor is a wonderful thing because it enables us to laugh at ourselves.

11. The speaker is reminded of a joke in closing.

With these golden words ringing in their heads the graduates go out from the ivied halls almost unable to walk under the burden of all that wisdom.

COMPULSORY RESTLESSNESS AMONG THE NATIVES . . .

Chancellor Samuel P. Dedicated of Gratuitous U. glanced through the dusty window of his book-lined study, rapped sharply on the glass and scowled at a group of students who had been sitting in the wan late-winter sunshine on the library steps.

They looked up, got to their feet, raised signs bearing such words as "Fight," "Yes," "No" and "However," and began walking glumly around the quadrangle.

Turning to a visitor, Doctor Dedicated explained, "It's a compulsory picketing class. Every student must have five hours of picketing before he can graduate, you know."

"The kids," he added cheerfully, "hate it."

The visitor, who had come to interview the silver-haired scholar as to why Gratuitous U. seemed to be an oasis of ordered calm as compared with the strife-torn campi of other universities, asked a question:

"Why does Gratuitous U. seem to be an oasis of ordered calm as compared with the strife-torn campi of other universities?"

The chancellor puffed thoughtfully upon his pipe before answering, "Compulsion is the key. You have just seen an example of how our students have come to detest picketing. In my long years as a silver-haired scholar and educational administrator I have learned that once anything on a college campus is made compulsory, the American student will do almost anything to avoid it.

"Being an ace scientist, in addition to those other things, I naturally tried it out first on white mice. When they were supposed to be doing something else, the white mice showed a great interest in running through mazes.

"When they were forced into the maze by electric shocks, however, they reacted the way I had suspected they might. They goofed off. It is a well-established fact that anything that works with white mice works with students. So when picketing was made compulsory the students goofed off just like the mice.

"There is even a theory among certain members of the faculty that picketing is in itself a form of goofing off from other compulsory activities. I should add that this is a minority view, albeit an interesting one.

"Our students now go to fantastic lengths to get out of picketing. They will say that they have forgotten their signs or lost them and their parents refuse to buy them new ones. Or they will present what purport to be notes from their family physicians saying that picketing is bad for their asthma, bursitis or some other fancied ailment."

Doctor Dedicated permitted himself a chuckle.

"At some schools," the visitor said, "there are problems involving undemocratic membership policies of the fraternities and sororities. Do these arise at Gratuitous U.?"

"We had a flurry of excitement in this field a few years ago," the chancellor conceded, "but there, too, we brought the theory of compulsion into play. We simply made it compulsory that every student belong to a fraternity or sorority.

"When the parents started getting the bills for the initiation fees and dues and when the students found that the food was punk and the beds lumpy, we were faced with an incipient revolt. There was mass picketing with signs such as 'Down With Compulsory Brotherhood' and 'Freedom Now.' We acceded to the demand, which we had expected all along, and restored the social organizations to their previous voluntary status. This solved the fraternity-sorority agitation but naturally gave a great impetus to picketing, which is when we instituted the compulsory picketing program."

"How about the dirty-word campaign that is rocking some institutions of higher learning?" the visitor asked. "Students are going around uttering four-letter words and worse, claiming that any policy of suppression would be an offense against their right of free speech."

"We have not yet encountered that problem," Doctor Dedicated replied, "but we are prepared. We would simply make dirty words compulsory, and I can promise you that, before long, the students would be going to almost any lengths to avoid them."

His secretary entered the office at this point and placed a bulky manuscript on the chancellor's desk.

"You see," he said to the visitor. "Here is a student petition demanding the abolition of compulsory picketing."

"What will you do about it?"

"Think it over," he said. "I am always willing to hear from the students. But whatever we do about compulsory picketing, there is one step that I definitely intend to take."

"And what is that?"

"It may be time to make petition writing compulsory," said the eminent educator as he smilingly bade the visitor good day.

✳ "And," Chancellor Dedicated added on the occasion of a later interview, "we are instituting a graduate course in Looting, which enables the entire Rioting program to be self-supporting. Where do you think I got this air conditioner and comfy chair?"

FROM A SAPLING IN THE GROVES OF ACADEME . . .

Sir:

I haven't been talking too much this week to my colleagues on the science faculty, but here in the humanities we feel that it is part of being a well-rounded man to keep up with what is doing over there in "stinks" which is what, in our undergraduate days, we used to call the chemistry place and whatever the other laboratories are.

After all, one can't be a well-rounded man in the twentieth century, can one, unless one knows something of the physical sciences. So I have made it a point to check a couple of scientific items in the press.

The first is datelined London, for some reason, although it comes in actuality from the University of Sydney in New South Wales. Its import is that it has finally been scientifically established that water glugging down the bathtub drain swirls clockwise in Australia, as opposed to counterclockwise in the northern hemisphere.

Everybody, even the liberal arts professors, has known this for years. Especially since the various foundations have been distributing grants and sending scholars on international trips so that the behavior of bathtub drains, if any, in any part of the world is no longer a mystery even to a man who teaches Chaucer.

At faculty teas, if an assistant professor announces that in his travels he has noted that the water glugs out in an opposite direction south of the equator the news is received with sneery looks to indicate that everybody knows that. It's about as big a bombshell as if an English instructor were to reveal that Shakespeare wrote with a goosequill pen.

What worries me, as a member of the academic community, is that the University of Sydney, presumably a semivenerable institution of learning, hadn't got around to finding out about this bath-drain phenomenon until long after it was common knowledge at East Pennsyltucky Normal.

What they did, according to the report in the press, was to let the water sit undisturbed in the bathtub "for at least eighteen hours, preferably longer." Then they pulled the plug and, *mirabile dictu,* there it swooshed out clockwise.

Somebody in New South Wales probably is getting a doctorate for pulling the plug.

The only explanation that occurs to me is that one of the big foundations gave a member of the physics faculty down under there a grant to come north for study. While here, apparently, he noticed the way the water ran out of the basin in his dorm at Harvard.

It was just like Ike Newton having his head appled. He went back to Australia and started his experiments. Those who laughed were silenced, we may well believe, when the eighteen-hour-old bathwater churned clockwise down the plumbing.

Another small scientific notation of the week comes from Harvard (where the water exits counterclockwise), and it tells how Dr. Elso S. Barghoorn—(Intrusion of impudent voice: "Elso Barghoorn sounds like water going out of a bathtub drain clockwise." Never mind.)

Doctor Barghoorn has evidence that there was a living organism on this planet three billion years ago. Not much of an organism, true. But an organism, nevertheless. A fossilized bacterium, to be exact, found in the microcrystalline chert in South Africa.

Good. I always like to hear about things being older than had been earlier thought, because it makes a man feel younger by comparison.

My only point is that the announcement of this discovery

"created a stir" at the Geological Society of America convention. As a humane letters man, I must ask, "How does one create a stir at a scientific convention?"

Do learned fellows exclaim "How about that?" or "Son of a gun!" or do they just stir about, like restless cattle?

I realize I have raised more questions than I have answered, but as Sir C. P. Snow has said, we have two cultures and one must try to understand the other.

> Sincerely
> Thomas H. Tenure.
> Assoc. Prof.

✱ A teacher friend says she hesitates to dictate the length of her students' hair, but it's hard to teach 'em if you can't see 'em.

BUY THE COLLEGE OF YOUR CHOICE . . .

In the mail comes a notice that a small California college is for sale. I can't think of anything nicer than to have one's very own college.

For one thing, all your gift problems would be solved. If a friend or relative had a birthday, was in the hospital, celebrating an anniversary or merely wanting to know that you were thinking of him, there would be no more trying to find a snappy greeting card, the perfect book or a suitable aspidistra.

Give him an honorary degree from You U.

Think of how a bachelor could impress his lady friend. To paraphrase the ad: "Promise her anything but give her a Ph.D."

The thrill of owning your own football team would be almost indescribable. And imagine your very own band spelling out your name at half-time and the privilege of composing the Alma Mater with your name in it just like John Harvard, Lord Jeffrey Amherst and Sam Wisconsin.

✳ Maybe the answer to Selective Service is to start everybody off in the Army and draft them for civilian life as needed.

DIG WE MUST, BUT DO WE DIG WHAT WE DIG?

At the annual meeting of the Universe Archaeological Society for the year 30,625,802 (Note to Editors: The Society uses the Standard Solar System calendar and you may wish to convert the date to the method of time computation used on your own planet. On Earth, for example, this would be 3965) this report on his recent excavations in the area known to the ancients as North America (planet Earth) was read by Professor YK 2 of the University of Eastern Mars:

"An extraordinarily productive dig was made in the fabled land of Outer Suburbia, about which we know little except what has come down to us in song and folklore. For many years, indeed, it was thought that the Suburbanites were mythical beings. We know now that they did exist, but the more we learn about them the more confusing their civilization (if it can be called that) becomes to the scholars of modern times.

"Each dwelling place or 'ranch,' for example, had beside it a ritual shrine upon which it is thought that burnt offerings were made to the powerful goddess Barbara Q and her consort, the mighty spear-thrower Shish Kabob.

"Most of the artifacts of this strange people have, of course, been lost, probably because they lived in the Plastic Age before man had developed the requisite skills for working in more durable materials, such as stone, iron and wood. The fact that they made some limited use of these materials, however, indicates that they may have been in a stage of transition to a more sophisticated and stable way of life. The impermanence of their handiwork, including their dwellings, suggests that they may have been a nomadic people, much like their contemporaries, the marauding Yankees, Pirates, Dodgers and Charlie O's, of whom evidence has been found in many formerly occupied sites across the entire land mass.

"So mysterious and enigmatic were these people that it was a rare find indeed when we uncovered an excavation which apparently had lain at one time underneath one of their dwelling places. Others may disagree, but I firmly believe it was what was called a 'basement' in what little of their literature has survived.

"By some freak of preservation, we found in almost perfect condition, the following articles: A hat of some sort of animal fur, with a tail attached; a circle or hoop of plastic; a board to which had been attached four small wheels; and a garment for the upper body with an inscription on the back, obviously a caste mark or tribal identification, i.e., 'Olympic Drinking Team.'

"Our expedition has named the site Genuine Davey, which was all that was legible of some writing affixed to the inner surface of the fur hat. The fact that the Suburbanites were wearing fur hats in this era may change the thinking of climatologists. The Ice Age must have lasted much longer in the vicinity of Genuine Davey than had been supposed.

"Doctor 3 Krnk agrees with me that the 'Olympic Drinking Team' tunic confirms the legends of orgies in Suburbia which have come to us in literary fragments which earlier researchers dismissed as apocryphal.

"As to the purposes of the plastic circle and the wheeled board, I must admit there is little agreement. If the Suburbanites were big enough to wear the shirt, they were too big to ride on the board.

"Professor Kdy Pincus of the University of South Jupiter puts forward the theory that the hoop and the board were children's toys or playthings. But then we all know that Professor Pincus is a kind of nut, lovable though he is. To end on a humorous note, the whole expedition broke into laughter when the professor scooted around the dig standing on the board and revolving the hoop around his hips. It was several minutes before we could bring ourselves to remind him that this was a scientific expedition. He apologized immediately with his customary sunny courtesy."

A FATHER'S PLEA . . .

Note slipped under the front door of a school on opening day:

"I don't know how to tell you what is in my heart. But today I am entrusting to your care someone who is infinitely precious to me. I remember when she was born, so helpless, so appealing. I remember her first step, her first word, her first tooth, all the other firsts.

"Always she has had Daddy beside her to kiss away the tears. Now she is your responsibility. She is a big girl. So big, and yet so vulnerable, I thought today as she strode bravely off to school. Her sensitivity, her gentleness, her inquiring mind, her very physical well-being are for you to nurture or to wound.

"She wants so much to make a good impression. She'd die— not really, but that is the kind of exaggeration she uses—if she knew I had written this to you. Maybe I shouldn't have. But she's such a nice girl, and she means so much to her mother and me.

"Would it hurt you to be a little extra kind to her? Give her a smile? When she makes a mistake, as she will, try to ignore it or at least give her another chance? She's really quite bright, you know.

"I know you are busy and won't have too much time to think about the happiness of one person, but I'd appreciate it if you would be understanding. She is so enthusiastic about school. She has been sharpening pencils and buying erasers and notebooks for a week.

"And remember this:

"It may make no difference to you that she's my daughter, kids, but she's *your teacher*. So take it easy, huh?"

✳ "Is the head of the house at home?" a salesman asks a young mother, who replies, "No, at the moment he's in kindergarten."

KINDLY QUIT CALLING THE PROFESSOR SONNY . . .

"I want it in my obituary," said the distinguished-looking gentleman in the gray tweed suit as he dipped a shrimp into the curry sauce, "that I was the oldest dropout in the long history of Riverside High School."

His wife beamed. Standing side by side they looked like one of those handsome couples who, in the ads, have retired joyously on three hundred dollars a month. Which, indeed, was what they were, although the sum, fortunately, was somewhat larger than that.

"Morgan," she said, "dropped out of high school at the age of sixty-seven. It caused quite a stir."

The gentleman, whose name was Morgan Trauma, deposited neatly on a plate the toothpick from which he had just removed the shrimp.

"I was, naturally, called in by my faculty adviser," he said, "who pointed out the cash value of a high school diploma over the years of my working life. He told me that automation hits the unskilled worker first and that I wasn't going to find it very rewarding, hanging around the malt shop, and maybe stealing hubcaps.

"I felt a little embarrassed for the poor chap, but after all he had his job to do, and I certainly didn't intend to make it more difficult by interrupting to suggest that his remarks, sound as they were, had very little relevance for a retired hardware executive already crowding his biblical allotment of years."

Morgan Trauma is one of the growing army of older people who return to high school or college campus to receive the diploma that they had never got around to in their youth.

The newspapers are full of such headlines as GRANDMOTHER IS VALEDICTORIAN or PROUD OF SHEEPSKIN AT 88. And we all salute the perseverance and scholarly attainments of these folks, and sympathize with them on the impatience with which they must sit through the Commencement address as the speaker gives them his fourteen or fifteen sure rules for success and tells them that the future belongs to them, the Class of 1968.

Still, Morgan Trauma may not be alone among those who have enrolled in high school at a late date and, for one reason or another, been unable to make it through to graduation.

Life is going to be increasingly onerous for those in middle years. You see one of these looking gaunt and haggard and ask what's the trouble.

"My mother," he replies, "doesn't understand improper fractions."

"No more she should," you reply indignantly, "a dear lady of her age."

"But she is flunking," he says. "Can you imagine what this does to me? The humiliation? And only last week everything seemed to be going so well. I went to open house and was so proud of Mother. Her finger painting was on display and her notebook had won the neatness award. Mother has always been neat. How do you tell your mother that she can't watch Dean Martin or stay out after ten o'clock until her grades improve?"

Another man speaks up.

"I told Dad," he says, "that if there was just one more of those notes from the teacher about him talking in class he couldn't have the car."

"That seems reasonable," you say. "After all, which is more important, an education or a set of wheels?"

"Exactly what I thought," says the man, "except that I should have known Dad would talk in class. He has spent fifty years talking in the office, at board meetings, at conventions, all over the world. He can't stop now. I realize that. Perhaps I was too harsh."

"Not at all," you put in. "The older generation needs discipline. He'll thank you for it later."

"I'm not so sure," he says.

"What do you mean?"

"Well, Dad says that if I take away the car he won't let me be president of the company any more."

It's a problem.

HOW ABOUT A BACHELOR OF SHYNESS DEGREE?

One thing we have to be careful about is poking fun at research projects. A certain amount of cheap hilarity can be gained by pointing a finger at the Government-subsidized investigation of the love life of the hoppy-toad, but it will pay off many times over if the information thus gleaned will keep your wife or other loved one from eloping with a hoppy-toad.

Now about the Office of Education giving the University of Illinois $5,000 to discover a cure for "performance anxiety," which is what keeps people from making speeches: I don't object because it's trivial, but because it is subversive and against the public interest.

The university will make a "study of 100 students who become extremely nervous and tense when called upon to speak in public."

In other words, $5,000 of my money, and yours, is going to be devoted to taking one hundred normal, decent children and "curing" them to the point where they will bounce to their feet the minute a shrimp cocktail is put in front of them.

There is not now, never has been, and never will be a shortage of public speakers in this country. The only performance anxiety exhibited by the folks at the head table is caused by the fear that they may not be called on for a few remarks.

If I were the Office of Education I would give $5,000 or more to a university to study one hundred students who love to speak in public and see if there weren't some way to scare them out of it.

AND IN CONCLUSION, CLASS, I'LL GO QUIETLY . . .

Fuzad el Nkrmh, popular local exchange student, was enchanted by the commencement address delivered at the school he has been attending.

"The man who made the speech," he said, "was such a nice man. I told him I was sorry."

"Sorry?" I asked. "Why sorry?"

"Why," said Fuzad el Nkrmh, "because he will be locked up for ten years. Is that not your custom?"

When I indicated that, for some reason, it was not, he explained that in his country all commencement speakers were immediately incarcerated.

"Very nice incarceration, of course," he said. "They have pleasant quarters, you know, and books and whatever else they need. But it is, after all, not the same as being completely free. Which is why I told the nice man I was sorry."

"I'm afraid I don't quite get the thinking behind this custom of yours," I said.

"It is very simple," he replied. "Our people believe in responsibility. If you save a man's life you must take care of him as long as you both live. So it is with the man who makes the speech to the graduating class. He is responsible for them. For ten years, anyway."

"You seem to take this form of oratory seriously in your land," I said.

"But of course," he said. "It is only logical. A man stands up and tells our youth that if they will come early to the job and work hard and sacrifice every third year's crop to the Sacred Hippopotamus they will be rich and happy. So."

"So?"

"So a man who tells these young people how to live their lives ought to be held responsible, don't you think?"

"It's an idea."

"I don't know whether it's an idea or not," said Fuzad el Nkrmh, "but it's a custom."

"What happens after ten years?"

"The class has a, well, what you call a reunion, no?"

"Yes," I said, "a reunion. Lots of fun with straw hats and potato salad and pictures of the children."

"With my people," Fuzad said, "the ten-year reunion is more serious. It is solemn. It is like a court of law. All the people who have heard the commencement speech ten years before get up and tell how it has been with them.

"The prisoner, that is the man who made the speech, sits in a sort of cage. If one member of the class gets up and says 'Yes,

I followed this man's advice and today I have two lovely wives and many boy children and one thousand gronches in the bank,' why everyone cheers and tosses flowers and pomegranates at the commencement speaker.

"But if the next one arises and says 'Alas. I did as this man said in his commencement address and my wife is ugly and all my children are girls and my muck-bean crop failed three years in a row and I have yet to break one hundred at golf,' why then the commencement speaker is pelted with stones.

"So the testimony goes on, and we hear which of the graduates has had great success and which are in poverty or perhaps in jail. Then, when everybody has been heard from, they average it all out, and if the man gave good advice and most everybody is happy and propserous, he is turned loose and given a bag of golden gronches and a nice apologetic plaque."

"But," I said, "what if the class hasn't done well?"

"Why," the popular local exchange student explained, "then he is sacrificed to the Sacred Hippopotamus under circumstances which are perhaps too difficult for the queasy Western stomach to digest."

"But," I protested, "if a man who makes a commencement speech knows he is going to be held accountable for how the members of the class turn out ten years later, why, nobody would make commencement speeches."

"Yes," said Fuzad el Nkrmh. "I'm happy to say that's the way it seems to work out."

RETREAT

✳✳✳✳

Familiar as the expression "half the battle" may be, we know that battles do not come in halves, any more than lives do. There is no pause for a change of equipment and an inspirational message from the coach.

If there is a point at which the battle is half won (or half over anyway), we are unaware of it at the time. Only in retrospect, which may or may not be allowed us, can we say on what day or hour we passed the halfway marker.

In a battle, as in a life, the scoreboard clock is never official. What may seem to us to be the beginning of the second half may, in the event, turn out to be the closing seconds.

If I write as though I had much experience with military battles, I do not intend to. I had a war once, but who hasn't? There were a few moments that I had laid by to tell my children if they asked, "What did you do in the war, Daddy?" But they never asked, and I have forgotten what it was I would have told them.

When the great captains publish their memoirs, I look in the index, but I never find my name.

Everybody should have his name in an index. And every book should have an index. Here, then, is the index to this one.

Index

THE END